Wars of Terror

Wars of Terror

BY
GABRIELE MARRANCI

Bloomsbury Academic
An imprint of Bloomsbury Publishing Plc

B L O O M S B U R Y
LONDON · OXFORD · NEW YORK · NEW DELHI · SYDNEY

Bloomsbury Academic

An imprint of Bloomsbury Publishing Plc

50 Bedford Square	1385 Broadway
London	New York
WC1B 3DP	NY 10018
UK	USA

www.bloomsbury.com

BLOOMSBURY and the Diana logo are trademarks of Bloomsbury Publishing Plc

First published 2016

British Library Cataloguing-in-Publication Data
A catalogue record for this book is available from the British Library.

ISBN: HB: 978-0-8578-5104-8
PB: 978-0-8578-5105-5
ePDF: 978-0-8578-5226-7
ePub: 978-0-8578-5106-2

Library of Congress Cataloging-in-Publication Data
A catalog record for this book is available from the Library of Congress.

Typeset by Deanta Global Publishing Services, Chennai, India
Printed and bound in India

Contents

1

Introduction

27 December 1985: 8.14 am, Leonardo da Vinci–Fiumicino Airport outside Rome, Italy. People are queuing at the ticket counters of Israel's El Al Airlines and Trans World Airlines – people who are ready for their holidays, business trips; some leaving home, others returning. There's the usual chattering, yawning and impatience. The clock marks 8.15 am. A shower of bullets, then an explosion, screams, blood and crying. Sixteen people are dead on the floor of the airport, ninety-nine are wounded, some fatally so. Among the dead lies an American diplomat named Wes Wessels. Three of the Palestinian terrorists were killed by the Italian police on the spot, and another would soon be arrested.

At 8.16 am on the same day, Schwechat airport, in Vienna, Austria, saw hand grenades thrown into crowds of passengers queuing to check in for a flight to Tel Aviv. Two innocent people were killed while thirty-nine were wounded. Overall, the two synchronized attacks claimed nineteen lives, including that of a child, and wounded more than 140 people. The coordinated terrorist attacks had the signature of Abu Nidal Organization, an extremely radical Palestinian group (Wege 1991).

A couple of months earlier, on 7 October 1985, four men declaring to be part of the Palestine Liberation Front (PLF) hijacked the MS *Achille Lauro* liner just off the Egyptian coast. The cruise destination was Ashdod, Israel. Before leaving the boat, they killed Leon Klinghoffer, an elderly American man in a wheelchair, and threw his body overboard. He was killed because he was a Jew.

In September 1986, in Karachi, Pakistan, a Pan American World Airways Boeing 747-121, Flight 73, was preparing for take-off when four men armed with Kalashnikovs and explosives hijacked the aircraft. The terrorists, four Palestinian men of Abu Nidal, wanted the flight to take off, but the captain managed to escape from the aircraft, leaving them unable to accomplish their plans for a suicide attack – that of crashing the plane into a prominent target in Israel. Three hours into the ensuing standoff, to show that they were 'serious' terrorists, they killed a passenger, their first victim. Sixteen hours later, while negotiations were ongoing, the auxiliary power unit that powered the plane's electrical system ran out, plunging the aircraft in darkness. Thinking that the Pakistani special forces were storming the aircraft, they ordered the passengers to go to the centre of the aircraft, whereupon they started to shoot and throw hand grenades at the passengers while screaming, 'jihad!' They killed twenty innocent passengers, of which twelve were from India and the rest from the United States, Pakistan and Mexico, and injured hundreds (Thexton 2006).

In October of the same year, a synagogue in the Karaköy quarter of Beyoğlu district, in Istanbul, Turkey, would see the first terrorist attack against a Jewish community since the formation of Turkey as a nation. Two gunmen, both Palestinians, opened fire during the Shabbat and killed twenty-two people – the Abu Nidal Organization appears to have carried out this attack too. A few years later, on the evening of 11 July 1988, the cruise ship *City of Poros*, carrying 400 passengers and seventy-one crew members, left the harbour. After the ship covered a few miles, at 8.30 pm, Palestinian gunmen, who had passed for tourists, opened fire with their automatic weapons and used grenades, killing nine tourists, fatally injuring two and severely injuring another ninety-eight. Abu Nidal, as usual, claimed responsibility for the action.

Pan Am Flight 103 was flying from Frankfurt to Detroit via London, when it exploded in the sky above the Scottish town of Lockerbie on 21 December 1988, killing all 243 passengers and sixteen crew members. The burning plane would kill eleven more on the ground as it fell on residential areas of the town. In 2003 Muammar Gaddafi admitted Libya's responsibility for the terrorist action and paid compensation to the victims' families, yet he denied being personally involved. Recently, the involvement of the Popular Front for the Liberation of Palestine-General Command (PFLP-GC) has been suggested. The militant organization has been responsible for other plots and attacks.[1]

In Algiers, Algeria, six years later, on 24 December 1994, a commando of Algerian terrorists – members of the Armed Islamic Group (GIA) – hijacked Air France Flight 8969 at Houari Boumedienne Airport with only one intention: to blow up the plane over the Eiffel Tower in Paris. The pilot diverted the plane to Marseilles, where the French special operations unit GIGN stormed the aircraft and killed all four hijackers, who had, sadly, already killed three passengers. On 25 July 1995, a gas bottle exploded in the Saint-Michel station of 'Line B' of the Réseau Express Régional (RER, Paris regional train network). The terrorist action killed eight and wounded eighty. On 17 August, a bomb exploded at the Arc de Triomphe, wounding seventeen people. Nine days later, on 26 August, a large bomb was found, fortunately undetonated, on the railroad tracks of a high-speed rail line to Lyon; had the bomb exploded, it would have been one of the most devastating terrorist attacks in the history of France. Yet, this was not the only time that Parisians were lucky. On 3 September of that same year, a bomb planted in a Paris square malfunctioned as it detonated and wounded four people – if it were not for this malfunction, the explosion would have resulted in a big tragedy. Later, these attacks were linked to Khaled Kelkal, whom the French gendarmerie killed on 29 September in a controversial operation that was recorded and later broadcast on TV. Kelkal was a juvenile delinquent who had served time in prison. While serving his sentence, he not only became radicalized, but also started to recruit Muslims for the Algerian civil war. After leaving prison in 1993, he visited his family in Mostaganem, Algeria, and probably joined the GIA, for which he organized the terrorist operation in France described above. Kelkal's death, however, did not stop the wave of Islamic terrorism ravaging France. On 6 October 1995, another gas bottle exploded in the Maison Blanche station of the Paris Métro, wounding thirteen, and on 17 October, a mere eleven days later, a gas bottle exploded between the Musée d'Orsay and Saint-Michel – Notre-Dame stations of RER 'Line C', wounding twenty-nine.

The next year, 1996, saw another series of attacks and plots, at least one of which was unsuccessful only by chance. These were organized by a new Islamic terrorist cell, which financed itself with a series of criminal endeavours – although most of these were intercepted by the police. Yet, on 28 March 1996, the group successfully parked a car with four gas tanks connected to a detonator next to a police station in Lille. The terrorist group had hoped to pulverize the entire building, but the bomb failed to explode in a big way and destroyed only the car. The attack occurred just two days before Lille hosted the G7 conference. Finally, the group was traced and the French anti-terrorist unit raided the house that it had operated from in spring 1996, when four members of the terrorist cell were killed; two had escaped and eventually found refuge in Bosnia. Apparently, this cell had the support of a very rich Saudi man whose family was very influential: Osama bin Laden.

*****

The accounts above summarize numerous instances of terrorist attacks and plots that were organized and executed by individuals and groups who identified themselves, and were identified by others, as Muslims. During the execution of the attacks, the perpetrators often uttered exclamations such as 'Allahu Akbar' or 'Jihad!'. Never again would Europe experience such frequency and intensity of what was called 'Islamic terrorism'. No politician, during those years, made any reference to 'war' or questioned the possibility that such actions may be a serious threat to the 'Western civilization'. The public, the political world, and scholars and analysts interpreted those acts of violence not very differently from how they understood and dealt with both communist-

and fascist-inspired terrorism, which ravaged 1960s'–1980s' Europe (Yonah and Pluchinsky 1992; Sprinzak 1995; Weinberg and Eubank 1988). Having asked the students in my courses, for the past three years, whether they knew of any of these terrorist actions or that so many terrorist attacks had taken place in Europe, I have noticed that only a few could mention, at the most, the Lockerbie bombing. For them, what has been labelled 'Islamic terrorism' is a new phenomenon that started with 9/11 and, with one man, Osama bin Laden.

Fast-forward to 11 September 2001 – the success of a plot, which terrorists for a long time had attempted to accomplish but for several lucky coincidences never achieved, would change world history. An aircraft was used as a missile against a Western target. Surely, this tragedy caused the highest loss of lives in a single day in the West due to a terrorist attack and, indeed, was the first attack on the United States since the attack on Pearl Harbor; this time, it was at the economic heart of the nation. Yet even such a devastating attack cannot completely explain the subsequent events, narratives and rhetoric which we today know as the *War on Terror*.

The War on Terror has marked the deepest changes in Western democratic countries since the end of the Second World War. Almost no aspect of ordinary life has been left unchanged: trade, transport and communications have suffered disruptions, in one way or another, as indeed have civil liberties (Shafir, Meade and Aceves 2012). Academics and human rights activists alike have highlighted the erosion of personal freedom and civil rights, as well as the demonization of communities, such as the Muslims, in particular, in the United States, Europe and Australia. Shafir et al. suggest in their analysis that, in the aftermath of 9/11, the Bush administration systematically created social panic through the emotive manipulation of the significance of the attacks and the power of al-Qaida and then, as we have witnessed in 2003, Saddam Hussein. In other words, what the Bush administration created and spread far beyond the United States is what Cohen has identified as 'political moral panic' (Cohen 2011). In a detailed study, Hetherington and Suhay (2011: 557) have shown that

> when ordinary people perceive a grave threat to their safety, they are susceptible to adopting antidemocratic preferences regardless of whether they score high in authoritarianism. In this rendering, antidemocratic preferences can quickly become popular, mainstream positions under the right circumstances. Indeed, to a certain extent, this has been the experience in post-9/11 America, with support for preemptive war, torture, wiretapping without warrant, and the like sometimes enjoying majority support.

Others, such as most of the European nations and Australia, started to introduce controversial anti-terrorism legislations (Mcdonald 2005; Tufail and

Poynting 2013). Terrorism per se, however, had little impact on everyday life, due to the rarity of attacks on Western metropolises, and when compared to previous waves of political and international terrorism (Merolla and Zechmeister 2009), the resulting changes to 'our way of life' were mainly political and introduced by the Western states themselves.

What has changed is that in the case of 9/11, the response to terrorism was not framed simply as a matter of dealing with criminality or terrorism, as in previous years, but rather has been developed through the concept of 'war'. The conceptualization is not even metaphorical, but rather,

> a real war waged on many fronts. … The characterisation of 9/11 as an act of war (rather than, as others have argued, a criminal act) and the response to terrorism as a 'war on terror' (rather than an investigation into terrorist crimes) is a discursive achievement. This achievement has naturalised one characterisation of 9/11 and America's response to terrorism as the dominant way to talk about the issue. (Hodges and Nilep 2007: 23)

This dominance will continue in the years to come even if the rhetoric, for instance, of President Obama, may have changed, with, in some cases, the word 'war' dropped from politicians' speeches concerning terrorism (McCrisken 2011; Pious 2011).

The use of the concept of 'war' is more than just a political narrative. In fact, it reveals a deeper discourse of values. The war is not against a state or even a rebellious group, and it is not even a 'civil war', despite the fact that the enemy is also represented as being 'within'. In his speech following the terrorist attack on the World Trade Center, President Bush made it clear to his nation and the world that despite the attack being an act of war, no conventional war would be waged:

> They were acts of war. This will require our country to unite in steadfast determination and resolve. Freedom and democracy are under attack. The American people need to know that we're facing a different enemy than we have ever faced. This enemy hides in shadows, and has no regard for human life. This is an enemy who preys on innocent and unsuspecting people, then runs for cover. But it won't be able to run for cover forever. This is an enemy that tries to hide. But it won't be able to hide forever. This is an enemy that thinks its harbors are safe. But they won't be safe forever. This enemy attacked not just our people, but all freedom-loving people everywhere in the world. (Bush 2001, September 12, quoted in Hodges and Nilep 2007: 25)

This, clearly, is a war in which values such as freedom, good, evil, justice, injustice and democracy and the dearest values derived from the Enlightenment are 'at stake'. Yet, this war does not have a temporal frame of years, but, rather, of generations: 'The war on terror is not a figure of speech. It is an inescapable calling of our generation' (Bush 2004, 19 March, quoted in Hodges and Nilep 2007: 30). This is a clash where the people of this generation will have to make themselves afraid for the good of humanity and civilization: 'We're on the offensive, we will not rest, we will not retreat, and we will not withdraw from the fight until this threat to civilization has been removed' (Bush 2006, 5 September, quoted in Hodges and Nilep 2007: 33).

Bush and his administration set the tone for an increasingly vivid narrative of civilizational clash, and other politicians would soon follow such rhetoric – from Tony Blair to Silvio Berlusconi to John Howard, as we shall see in Chapter 2. The war was seen as a civilizational war, and one that may decide the fate of the democratic West. This civilizational narrative was repeated in newspapers, TV talk shows, websites of different kinds and in popular books (Croft 2006; Holloway 2008). One of the most popular books that reacted to the events of 9/11 was *The Rage and the Pride*, which sought to be 'a j'accuse ... a prosecution or sermon addressed to Europeans. [It was] an unrestrainable cry' (Fallaci 2002: 21) and sold over one million copies in Italy alone, and topped the bestseller list for several months, even surpassing books such as *The Da Vinci Code* and the *Harry Potter* series.[2] Fallaci, despite being disliked by intellectuals and academics for her demonization of Muslims and Islam, was able to resonate with many men and women in Western capitals for whom the catchphrase 'Bush's War on Terror' had become 'common sense'. Fallaci expressed in her book the fears that are at the heart of the War on Terror and, at the same time, that feeling of rediscovering a 'civilizational pride' that after 9/11 was rapidly spreading as much as the fear of Muslims and the hatred of Islam. Her words, in *The Rage and the Pride*, are clear and dramatic:

> You don't understand, you don't want to understand, that a Reverse Crusade is underway. A war of religion they call Holy War, Jihad. You don't understand, you don't want to understand, that for those Reverse Crusaders the West is a world to conquer and subjugate to Islam. (Fallaci 2002: 27)

A man in an orange boiler suit kneels, while another man, in black 'ninja-style' clothes with a knife in his hand, stands close by. The orange suit resembles those that detainees wear in Guantanamo, and just like those men, the one on his knees is a prisoner too. His name is James Foley and he had been held captive for two years in Syria before mysteriously ending up in IS's murderous hands (Islamic State, formerly ISIS). In a barbaric ritual seen repeatedly in al-Qaida videos, the journalist and video reporter Foley blames, in his final words, the United States for having 'signed' his 'death certificate'. Then, before the knife reaches Foley's throat, the executioner addresses the United States and, with it, the entire West, in crisp British-accented words:

> You are no longer fighting an insurgency; we are an Islamic Army and a state that has been accepted by a large number of Muslims worldwide, so effectively, any aggression towards the Islamic State is an aggression towards Muslims from all walks of life who have accepted Islamic Caliphate as their leadership. So any attempt by you, Obama, to deny the Muslims their right of living in safety under the Islamic Caliphate will result in the bloodshed of your people.[3]

Foley's beheading shocked Western audiences, both Muslim and non-Muslim. The barbaric actions of the self-proclaimed Islamic State appear, if such a thing is possible, to be even more bloodthirsty than those of al-Qaida.

Has Samuel Huntington's prophesy materialized in full? Is this a 'clash of civilisations' (1993), as the emphatic title of Huntington's article suggested nearly ten years before Bush declared the War on Terror? Osama bin Laden, as we shall see in Chapter 2 of this book, strongly thought so. This was not a war against nations, nor was this jihad against one dar-al-harb,[4] this was, according to those whom I will describe as *civilizers*, a global conflict. This was a struggle for the hegemony of values, ethos and the correct way of being human.

Huntington's theory of the clash of civilizations, in reality, is more than just an academic theory – it is, even in more sophisticated prose than that of Oriana Fallaci, a rallying call to the West to realize the danger it faces as far as identity is concerned:

> The 'West' was not simply a geographical community but a universalistic creed of individualism, liberalism, constitutionalism, human rights, democracy, and free markets. It is simultaneously a real place and an imaginary cultural order. 'The West versus the Rest' is not simply a spatial struggle between a distinct 'here' (the West) and an identifiable 'there' (the Rest), but a cultural and spatial struggle that occurs everywhere. (O'Tuathail 1996: 247)

O'Tuathail could not have been more right in his analysis of Huntington's understanding of the West. Through a deterritorialized presentation of the West in the rhetoric of the 'War on Terror', actors try to 'discipline the real to fit the imaginary' (O'Tuathail 1996: 248) – an imaginary that will be a central discourse of this book.

As readers may have noticed, this book is titled *Wars of Terror* instead of *War on Terror*. Indeed, it is not the intention of this book to discuss the events of this now lengthy, unstable geopolitical period; it is also not the intention of this book to offer a traditional political reflection on the War on Terror and its aftermath; nor is it the intention to discuss recent developments, although they will be taken into consideration and are part of the narrative of this book. The reason this book does not focus on such aspects is that there is enormous academic and, even more so, popular literature that focuses on the War on Terror, Islamic terrorism, jihad and so forth. Just to provide you with an idea, at least an astonishing 5,153 academic books have been published with the above-mentioned phrases in the title since 2002, as well as at least 9,362 journal articles[5] – and this collection is ever growing.[6]

This book's intention, instead, is to provide a different understanding of why we are witnessing what can be defined as *wars of terror*. Indeed, if the phrase 'war on terror' seems to ethnocentrically (Kam and Kinder 2007), or better western-centrically, focus on the fear, perceptions of threat and insecurities of western nations, with *wars of terror*, I intend to focus on the dynamics of fear which push some individuals to adopt a civiliser *forma mentis* – a particular way of thinking about, imagining and reacting to the environment, its challenges and its threats. In the wars of terror, which are not always fought with weapons, there are no opposing categories of Muslim and non-Muslim, but rather only humans, humans who have strong faith, not just in religious and political ideals, but also in deeper sentiments from which both these ideals are derived. They believe they know *how to be human* and they want to impose this knowledge on others, since if they fail to do so, they run the risk of having their own idea of humanity threatened.

This circle of panic induces a civilizational discourse and rhetoric that have an ontological aspect: those who are on the other side of the civilizational divide are dehumanized – they are not seen as being *properly* human – and are often referred to, instead, as a category – as the barbarian, the Muslim, the Westerner, the Christian, the jihadi, the crusader, the uncivilized, the *kuffar*, the pig, the dog, the Shaytan, the evil or the terrorist. The wars of terror aim to obliterate inhumanity so that only humans can exist, who are, of course, the *correct* kind of humans. How such 'sub-humans' are obliterated varies from drones to bombs, to denial of rights, to persecutions and so on. Dehumanization is a central focus of this book. Although the social sciences have studied the processes of dehumanization for a long time, the research remains fragmented and lacks a systematic theoretical framework. As Haslam (2006) has noticed, references to dehumanization can be found in studies focusing on ethnicity (Jahoda 1999), race, migration and genocide (Chalk and Jonassohn 1990; Kelman 1976). Psychological studies have provided most of the theoretical discussion on dehumanization, and Haslam (2006) has provided a review of the main theoretical approaches. He has, for instance, highlighted the relevance of Bar-Tal's (2000) *delegitimising beliefs*, in which extremely negative characteristics are projected onto the out-group with the aim of denying the humanity of its members. Relevant to the argument I am proposing, Haslam has suggested that 'delegitimizing beliefs share extremely negative valence, emotional activation (typically contempt and fear), cultural support, and discriminatory rejection of the outgroup' (2006: 254).

Values, and what I will refer to in Chapter 3 as ethos, according to Struch and Schwartz (1989), are an important factor in dehumanization, since 'beliefs about a group's value hierarchy reveal the perceiver's view of the fundamental human nature of the members of that group' (and Struch and Schwartz 1989, quoted in Haslam 2006: 225). If the out-group is considered an antagonist in terms of values, it is identified as lacking in humanity. A very important concept that has recently developed is the so-called *infra-humanization*. Leyens et al. (2003) (but see also Leyens et al. (2001)) have demonstrated with a series of laboratory studies that people attribute more unique secondary human emotions to their own group than primary emotions; primary emotions, which humans share with animals, are attributed to members of out-groups. It was also shown in another study (Gaunt, Leyens and Sindic 2004) that since the in-group tends not to attribute secondary emotions to the out-group, it tends not to help the individuals of the out-group who may express secondary emotions that demonstrate a particular need. According to Haslam, infra-humanization is interesting since it 'is not reducible to in-group favouritism (both positive and negative secondary emotions are denied to out-groups). Infra-humanization also occurs in the absence of intergroup conflict, and therefore extends the scope of dehumanization well beyond the context of cruelty and ethnic hatred' (2006: 255).

In Chapter 2, we shall focus on the concept of civilization and its history from both Western and non-Western perspectives. We will observe how the concept has been used as part of a rhetoric aimed at differentiating societies and cultures. As Casanova (2005) has highlighted, although Huntington has dismissed the illusion of a hegemonic *Pax Americana* after the end of the Cold War, and identified a new basis – different values – of conflict, his analysis is overly essentialist and scholars have correctly pointed out several flaws. However, while Huntington may have essentialized the concept of civilization, it is also indeed demonstrable, as Starobinski (1993: 30) observes, that the idea of a civilizational conflict has made people feel compelled to take sides, 'adopting' the causes of the civilization that one belongs to and rejecting anything that is perceived as a threat, inevitably tagging it as 'absolute evil'. As we will discuss in Chapter 2, the clash is not between geo-religious ontologies, but rather the clash is of civilizational narratives set against the backdrop of frequent calls for 'purity', where the globalizing world is perceived as a threat that may dilute one's own values and, with them, one's existence (Douglas 1988).

In Chapter 3, after reviewing some anthropological studies that try to explain the current tensions between Muslims and non-Muslims, as well as reactions to the concept of 'secularism', so central to the resistance of some Muslim groups, we will focus on the 'tools' that civilizers use in their efforts to delegitimate the other. Stereotypes and stigmatization are identified as essential to the process of dehumanization. After analysing the concept of ethos, particularly from an anthropological understanding, we will explain how the ultimate goal of any civilizer is that of defining the ethos of his or her own group and to define who is properly 'human', as well as how, in doing so, civilizers can even use violence against their own nation or group, like in the case of terrorist Anders Behring Breivik in Norway. The reason for such in-group violence could be explained as a desperate attempt to punish what the civilizer sees as a betrayal of ethos, where violence is an act to correct his or her own group and to remove the risk of threat from the 'un-ethical' other.

In Chapter 4, we focus on the rhetoric of delegitimization and on the discourse on civilization. 'Islamophobia' is increasing in Western countries, and this has been well documented in both mass media and academic literature. However, trying to understand the 'fear of the West' among some Muslims holds no such advantage as there is a clear lack of studies and research in this area. After engaging in a discussion of such phenomena, we go on to explore one of the most important aspects behind the 'wars of terrors': conspiracy theories. There are very few studies that discuss conspiracism among Muslims; even among them some are affected by ideological preconceptions about Muslims. Yet, it is evident that conspiracies are central to the continuation of the wars of terror as well as to the main way in which civilizers, from both sides, recruit others to their cause. Among the concepts that are linked to ethos but also to conspiracism among some Muslims is the rhetorical usage of *jahiliyya* (pre-Islamic way of life). The fear of *jahiliyya*, expressed in words or in an indirect fashion, is central to the fear of the West. Similarly, sharia has become a central topic in the mass media of Western countries, in which civilizers use the concept to heighten the fear that Muslims can change the secular and democratic way of life that is so central to the ethos of Western civilizers.

In Chapter 5, we observe how gender is part of the clash of civilizers. After a review of how women have been central to the narrative of civilization for centuries, we see how, today, the rhetoric about women's issues has become part of the wars of terror. Yet, again, we will see that there is a lack of academic literature about the views of Muslim civilizers concerning Western and secular women. In this chapter, we seek to provide a glimpse into the rhetoric of such civilizers who see themselves as the saviours of Western women through Islam, something parallel and opposite to those who perceive themselves to be Judeo-Christian civilizers on a mission to 'save' Muslim women from the veil and sharia.

In Chapter 5, we, however, highlight another, surely understudied and recent, aspect of the use of gender in civilizer discourse. Just like women, non-heterosexual people have become part of the discourse of civilization. In Muslim countries, and among many Muslims living in the West, non-heterosexuality is often considered to be the consequence of a lack of correct ethos in the West, and a real disease that may affect Muslims through what many identify as 'Liberal Islam'. For non-Muslim civilizers, gays and lesbians must be saved from the sharia. We underline the contradiction that the same people who are most vocal in calling themselves the defenders of the alleged Judeo-Christian civilization also often tend to oppose gay rights in their own countries and express, more often than not, homophobic ideas.

In Chapter 6, we discuss the most violent aspect of the clash of civilizers – those who would like to begin a crusade against all Muslim countries and those who identify themselves as jihadis. We start by discussing in depth the case of the white supremacist and self-defined crusader Anders Behring Breivik, who explained his terrorist actions as a desperate attempt to save his 'Judeo-Christian civilization'. Then, I will discuss an example from my own fieldwork; the case of Younes Tsouli, better known as Irhabi 007. Through these examples, I explain that emotions and psychological processes have an essential role to play in the violent acts that are most often perpetrated against civilians and performed by civilizers. Then, I will suggest a theoretical framework that draws first on Antonio Damasio's understanding of emotions and feelings, then on recent studies on general strain theory, and finally on an exploration of the role that cognitive dissonance can play in providing an explanation of such violent acts. In the case of Muslims involved in terrorism, we will remind readers through this chapter that it would be wrong to consider them non-Muslims or not real Muslims and their radical views of Islam as 'non-Islam'. Islamic scholars, as of today, disagree on how to understand Islam, and no central authority exists that can provide a definitive understanding. To decide, as an anthropologist, who is a real Muslim would require one to enter the domain of theology. Rather, I suggest in this final chapter that Muslim civilizers do not see their religion as operating within a theological framework, but as a set of beliefs mediated through the processes that I have explained above. I have called this set of beliefs 'emotional Islam'.Notes

Notes

1 Jon Swaine, CIA held Syrian militants responsible for Lockerbie bombing, The Telegraph, 20 December 2013, http://www.telegraph.co.uk/news/worldnews/northamerica/usa/10532134/CIA-held-Syrian-militants-responsible-for-Lockerbie-bombing.html (accessed 12 October 2014).

2 http://observer.com/2003/01/the-rage-of-oriana-fallaci/ (accessed 12 October 2014).

3 http://thedailybanter.com/2014/08/breaking-isis-releases-youtube-video-executing-missing-american-journalist-james-foley/#AugU4cXgE7cv5MF8.99 (accessed 12 October 2014).

4 Traditional Islamic geopolitics divided the world into three major diplomatic entities: dar-al-Islam, or the lands under the control of Muslims, dar-al-harb, the lands under the control of non-Muslims and with whom no treaty was possible, and dar-al-amn, the land where Muslims were allowed to practise their religion, even if Islamic law was not established as state law.

5 This very rudimental data has been derived from checking the online Worldcat catalogue, https://www.worldcat.org/ (accessed 12 October 2014).

6 See for instance, Durham (2015), Cockburn (2015) and Delphy (2015).

2

The concept of civilization: From abstraction to a new common sense

Why is it important to explore the historical and social development (i.e. *Begriffsgeschichte*) of the concept of 'civilization'? Concepts have a historical trajectory, a proper development, which is not isolated from the events and environment in which they have been developed and discussed. Both events and the environment are part of their genealogy and dynamics. Reinhard Koselleck (1985: 74) has suggested that a concept has two functions: on the one hand, it signifies in the signification process (i.e. being linked to words); on the other hand, it gains layers of meanings according to its use (i.e. being linked to social usage). Concepts tend to move from scholarly to general usage and they become often used in the context of conflicts and polemics (Hampsher-Monk, Tilmans and van Vree 1988). The concept of civilization follows exactly such a trajectory, from being a technical word to having a general, nearly commonsensical meaning; yet not only does the conceptual history of 'civilization' show its ambiguities but it also shows its development as an epistemological weapon. In this chapter we shall follow such developments, and we shall observe the resurgence of the concept of civilization as a post-9/11 rhetoric.

Civilization: A conceptual history

Braudel, in his *A History of Civilisations*, claims, 'It would be pleasant to be able to define the word "civilisation" simply, and precisely, as one defines a straight line, a triangle or a chemical element' (Braudel 1994: 55). However, the concept of civilization, as suggested above, can be observed genealogically (i.e. through the lenses of history and development) and sociopolitically (i.e. semiotic power in contexts). The main function of the term 'civilization' continues, till today, to be: the capacity to differentiate. As such, although not a direct etymology to 'civilization', the ancient Greek βα' ρβαρος (barbarous) is critical to its conceptual development. The origin of 'barbarous' can be traced to the Homeric 'bar-bar', probably a derogatory onomatopoeic reference to the ancient Carian language, which Homer perceived as being childish and filled with gibberish. The meaning of the word 'barbarian' can be said to have crystallized after the victory of the Persians in the Persian War of 480–479 BC. The barbarian now was the foreigner, the non-Greek, the enemy, the unsophisticated, those who lacked recorded history, cities and laws (see Mazlish 2004: 3, 19–20). As Todorov has noticed, in the sixteenth century 'the tension between the two possible meanings of "barbarian", between the relative (a foreigner we cannot understand) and the absolute (a cruel person), was to become significant again' – this during 'the great voyages undertaken by the Europeans, who sought to classify populations of whose existence they had hitherto been unaware' (2010: 30).

For the proper etymology of *civilization*, however, we need to move from ancient Greece to ancient Rome. The Latin *civis* (citizen), which, in turn, derived from *civites* (city), is the antecedent of our term (Simpson and Weiner 1989). Now, while the βα' ρβαρος of the Greeks had a linguistic derivation, the Romans emphasized a different value. The Latin term *civites* is connected to *civitas* (*pl. civitates*), which in republican Rome was used to indicate that the citizens were united under the law, which gave them *munera*, or responsibilities (see Wood 1991). In other words, *civis* expresses, at the same time, geographical and sociopolitical values, whose ontology resides in the idea of urban space as the centre of culture and knowledge. To put it another way, 'It concerns the Roman use of the terms *cultus* and *cultura* (it is noteworthy that the Greeks had no such term, referring only to *paideia*, or what would later be called *Bildung* [culture] in German)' (Mazlish 2004: 21). Science, love for the arts, respect for the law and sophistication in the social construct of civil life made a Roman, according to the Romans, different from a barbarian. Such thinking, however, has another profound aspect: inevitable development of perceptions on 'uncultured', 'cultured' and 'culturable'. As Mazlish has observed, 'in this development is a future confusion between the terms "civilisation" and "culture"' (2004: 21).

In German you can indeed find two words, although different, expressing the same idea – *Kultur* and *Zivilisation*, where the former has a positive meaning compared to the latter – *Zivilisation* 'means something which is indeed useful, but nevertheless only a value of the second rank, comprising only the outer appearance of human beings, the surface of human existence' (Elias 1978: 6).

The two terms are related in another way. Despite the difference between 'civilization' as a universal state of humanity [i.e. *Zivilisation*] and a 'civilization' [*Kultur*] based on the supremacy of culture (Bowden 2004), the idea of supremacy remains the minimum denominator for both. It is not surprising that some scholars, such as Kuper (1999), have even suggested that Germany perceived the First World War as nothing other than the inevitable clash between the French/European *Zivilisation* and a very German *Kultur*.

If *Kultur* as a concept has an archaic pedigree, civilization was an eighteenth-century neologism which substituted the dichotomy between the civilized and the barbaric. Jean Starobinski has suggested that we can trace the first non-juridical usage of the concept of civilization to Victor Riqueti Mirabeau's 1756 *L'Ami des Homes* (1993). Starobinski (1993) has also highlighted an internal contradiction in the eighteenth-century debate on civilization: in a time in which intellectuals attempted to remove any influence of religion in their debate, Mirabeau suggested that the main source of civilization resides in religion, in that it is the latter that has educated individuals on politeness and respect. The tension inherent in the conceptualization of civilization as a secular tool of progress and yet, at the same time, as rooted in religious (i.e. Christian) values will remain permanent ; it is expressed even in sociology – in Weber's theory of capitalism (Weber 2002) and, in more recent times, Huntington's theory of the clash of civilizations (1996).

The neologism 'civilization' connects also to the process of modernization. In modernization's early stages, Europe was witnessing expansion and change as well as the industrial revolution (Weinner 1973). Many aspects in the customs and morals of the European society were changing, particularly, of course, among the most privileged classes. Among those considered 'civilized', good manners, improved status of women and secularism were often discussed. Mill, in 1817, argued, 'The condition of the women is one of the most remarkable circumstances in the manners of nations. Among the rude people the women are generally degraded; among the civilised people they are exalted' (Mill and Thomas 1975).

Of course, considering the limited rights that even noble women had at the time of Mill, such a comment may provoke a smile in the reader. Yet, Mill's reference to the condition of women was derived from the colonial experiences and reports of the lives of women in colonized countries such as India. The reference to women in the context of colonial rhetoric about civilization (see Boddy 2007; Rajan 2004; Gaitskell 1998) is another theme that, as we shall see in this book, would have strong implications up to our day, particularly in the function that it had in providing 'a standard by which to judge societies, and during the nineteenth century, Europeans devoted much intellectual, diplomatic, and political energy to elaborating the criteria by which non-European societies might be judged' (Huntington 1996: 41). In

Europe, civilization soon became a term to measure otherness, particularly, the archetype of difference, the Islamic other, represented by the Ottoman Empire.

Indeed, historians and other intellectuals suggested the Roman Empire as the genealogy of the idea of the West and its continuation within the historical development of the Christian Byzantine Empire as well as the *Sacrum Romanum Imperium* (The Holy Roman Empire). Therefore, the idea of the West was regarded not merely as a geographical or geopolitical dimension but rather as filled with 'traditional religious and political connotations ... [which] were, fitfully, being put to use to interpret Europe's rise to global power' (Bonnett 2004: 25). Indeed, we cannot analyse the concept of the West and its modern historical developments as a simple sociopolitical category. Instead, as Bonnett (2004) has argued, the very idea of the West provided a tool to hierarchically differentiate cultures and human societies. The contact with different cultures and the evaluation of such cultures based on ethnocentric judgements convinced the white Europeans of the superiority of 'White civilisation' (Bonnett 2004: 14). White supremacism informed the rhetoric and actions of colonialism as well as the discrimination of non-white minorities such as the African Americans in the United States. With the development of civil rights movements and sociopolitical battles against discrimination based on skin colour, the rhetoric declined and white solidarity started to fade, although it never disappeared entirely. Nonetheless, 'the idea of the West helped resolve some of the problematic and unsustainable characteristics of white supremacism' (Bonnett 2004: 36) and what had appeared to have left through the door entered through the window.

The rhetoric of modernization, together with the presumed superiority of the 'white man's science', similarly, can be traced from the white supremacism discourse of the old to the new modern concept of the West. Yet, the social changes that began in the 1950s, and in particular the 1960s, created a sense of insecurity for whiteness. The independence movements in Africa and Asia, the 1980s' collapse of the Soviet Union, the end of the Cold War, as well as the rise of the Asian Tiger states all created insecurity in the West and speculation about the role of the West in a new geopolitical order. The first perception was that the West was in retreat and later the perception was that it was endangered. It is here that a new reference to Western civilization developed through a new, and this time 'a-historical', powerful myth, the 'Judeo-Christian' roots of the Western civilization. Again the main reason for such a shift, that saw the return of religion as part of the definition of the West as a civilization, was to create differences within a reshaped world where values change at an incredible speed. The concept of civilization entered the stage again by conceiving the West as a Judeo-Christian civilization, which, however, was reduced to a sort of Weberian force, rather than a theological entity, since secularism remains the main marker of Western civilization and a prominent, as we shall see, weapon of the 'verbal arsenal of praise and blame' (Starobinski 1993: 29). During the Cold War, for instance, 'Christianity was constantly appealed to as something that helped define the West against the atheistic menace of communism' (Bonnett 2004: 3) in a simplified rhetoric of 'good and evil'. In fact, Starobinski has correctly observed that,

> Civilization itself becomes the crucial criterion: judgement is now made in the name of civilisation. One has to take its side, adopt its cause. For those who answer its call it becomes ground for praise. Or, conversely, it can serve as a basis for denunciation: all that is not civilisation, all that resists or threatens civilisation, is monstrous, 'absolute evil'. (1993: 30)

In 1989 the idea of 'absolute evil', at least at a political level, collapsed together with the Berlin Wall. The end of the communist regimes meant, according to many, that the 'West' had no rivals or enemies left and could guide the world towards prosperity and, in particular, freedom, helping it pass through modernism and secularism.

In these years what has been called *Pax Americana* (see Alasuutari 2004; Hurrell 2005) appears to have become a reality, with another new element, global democracy, and its consequence, democratization, revitalizing both the idea of civilization and civilizational efforts. Although not expressed in traditional colonial rhetoric, some neo-conservative intellectuals linked democracy to the idea of a superior civilization. As part of such a discourse, human rights, and in particular the rights of women, entered the equation. Some scholars and politicians, also influenced by the rather radical ideas of Leo Strauss (Pangle 2006), argued that Western civilization – according to these scholars and politicians the highest expression of which is the United States and its democracy – could expect to face resistance from another 'civilization'. Freed from the communist yoke, it would fight Western values, particularly democracy, and even attempt to destroy them (see Huntington 1996). Unsurprisingly, the main enemy was not a new one, but one which, as we have seen, had a long history in the process of shaping the European conceptualization of civilization: the dissolved Ottoman Empire. Yet, it was not Turkey or any other nation of the former empire that was to be singled out as the antagonist of Western civilization, it was Islam itself: 'What has changed since the collapse of Soviet communism is not the secularity of the West (the USA remains, relative to many East Asian societies, a notably religious country) but the rise of a new, religiously defined, opponent in Islam' (Bonnett 2004: 3).

In trying to understand the European *Begriffsgeschichte* of 'civilization', we have gone a full circle. In 1736, one of the most prominent European philosophers and intellectuals, Voltaire, represented Islam – at the time it was embodied in the geopolitical power expressed by the Ottoman Empire – in his *Le fanatisme, ou Mahomet le Prophete*, as anti-Enlightenment and anti-civilization; in the aftermath of 9/11, Bush expressed again the idea of a moral struggle, which saw the United States being forced to 'wage a war to save civilization, itself' (George W. Bush, 9 November 2001).[1]

The concept of civilization in the West had a complex yet defined intellectual trajectory. Is there a similar concept in the Islamic tradition? The simple answer is, yes, the English word civilization can be translated as *hadara* in Arabic. This, however, does not tell us very much about the intellectual trajectory within the Islamic tradition of the idea of civilization. If we open the Qur'an, the main sacred text of Islam, we do not find a specific word for 'civilization'; rather the Qur'an – in contexts where it clearly refers to what we call civilization – employs *qarya* that can be translated as a town or city. Again, as in the first forms of Western conceptualization, the meaning of civilization is convened through the difference between the urban, as a culturally modified space, and the non-urban, as a nature-controlled environment. Yet, it is not *qarya* that became popular as the Arabic translation of 'civilisation', but rather *hadara*, a term that Ibn Khaldun – the famous Arab social historian – introduced in 1377 in his monumental work *al-Muqaddimah* (Ibn Khaldun 1986).

Hadara means 'presence as opposed to absence' but also 'sedentary' as opposed to 'bedouin'; but it is also related to the word *hadhirah*, which means city or larger community, as well as the idea of constructing a large building (Ibn Manzur 1968: 4, 196–7 quoted in Benlahcene 2004). Ibn Khaldun argued that civilization was exclusively a human characteristic involving social pacts and social supports in order to satisfy human needs (1986: 84).

Nonetheless, *hadara* is not the only term for civilization; in the al-*Muqaddimah*, for instance, we can also encounter '*umran*', as in '*umran hadari*' (urban civilization). Other relevant Arabic terms are *madaniyah*, *nahdhah* and *tamaddun*, all referring to the idea of 'city' life contrasted with bedouin life. Until the nineteenth century, the preferred terms were '*umran* and *hadara*, but with the prolonged contact with Europeans, *madaniyah*, and its direct synonym *tamaddun*, seemed to have replaced Ibn Khaldun's terms. The term *madaniyah* has a religious connotation since its root is related to Medina, the city that Muhammad reached when he had to leave Makkah (the so-called *hegira*) and which not only marks the beginning of the Muslim calendar, but is also the birth of the first-known constitution, the Constitution of Medina (Lecker 2004). In other words, *madaniyah* refers to the act of providing law and order under the auspices of God's revelation. It is not surprising that revivalist Islamic writers have a preference for both *madaniyah* and *tamaddun* (the latter is used more commonly by non-Arab Muslims). As early as the second quarter of the twentieth century, however, *hadara* became the main term for civilization. Muslims for whom Arabic is not a mother tongue still use various terms that are derived from Arabic, as Beg has noticed (Beg 1982: 20). Again the roots of those words refer to 'city' as a synecdoche of 'culture' as opposed to that of nature.

We can conclude that the concept of 'civilization' that developed within the Muslim intellectual tradition shows some similarity to that which developed in the European one. Indeed, both are derived from the differences between nature and nurture, with culture, understood as the urban, becoming a mark of superiority. But European history has modified the Western concept of civilization by adding layers of new meanings; moral values and judgements were, for instance, not present in the traditional Muslim understanding of foreign civilizations. For Muslim authors such as Ibn Khaldun, civilization is not per se linked to any particular religion; this is unlike the European understanding which saw civilization being increasingly linked to Christianity, with the religion seen as a civilizational force even in those states where the doctrine of secularism was upheld.

9/11 and the conceptual resurgence of civilization

'We wage a war to save civilisation, itself' (Bush, 8 November 2001)[2]; 'Civilisation, itself, the civilisation we share, is threatened' (Bush, 11 November 2001).[3] There is no doubt that in the aftermath of 9/11 the words civilization and civilized had found a new resurgence. Since the end of colonialism and its 'civilizational' enterprise, no head of the state has employed the term 'civilization' as Bush and later Blair, together with a number of Western leaders, have. This was not because the shock felt over the terrorist act provoked a temporary emotional rhetoric, rather it marked the apotheosis of the New World Order discourse, which George W. Bush's father inaugurated (Lazar and Lazar 2004). As Collet (2009), through a careful analysis of a corpus of US presidential speeches that spans three years (from 2001 to 2004) has demonstrated, such discourse of civilization derives from a deeply held vision of the world, a vision first shaped within some academic and political environments. For instance, Bernard Lewis in *The Roots of Muslim Rage* argued that after the end of the Cold War, the main source of conflicts between what monolithically he identified as the West and Muslims, should not be found, for instance, in the impact that colonialism had on Muslim countries or in Middle East conflicts; rather, 'the fundamental source of conflict in this new world will not be primarily ideological or primarily economic. The great divisions among humankind and the dominating source of conflict will be cultural. ... The fault lines between civilisations will be the battle lines of the future' (1990: 22).

Although Bernard Lewis coined the term 'clash of civilisation' (Gilpin 2005), Samuel Huntington first provided the theoretical framework first in his seminal article 'The clash of civilizations?' (Huntington 1993), where a timid question mark left a door open for debate. Then, three years later, in his most cited book, *The Clash of Civilizations and the Remaking of World Order* (Huntington 1996), little doubt was left as to the developments that the post-Cold War world would witness; the author reinforced the view that culture, as expressed by religion, was central to the most disruptive, but also ultimate, conflict. For Huntington, just as for many who support his analysis, the Judeo-Christian (i.e. Western) civilization is superior and should prevail.

Huntington suggested that the clash has two different levels: 'At the micro level, adjacent groups along the fault lines between civilisations struggle, often violently, over the control of territory and each other. At the macro-level, states from different civilisations compete for relative military and economic power, struggling over the control of international institutions and third parties, and competitively promote their particular political and religious values' (Huntington 1993: 29). Huntington connected his clash of civilisations to those few scholars who suggested (Alasuutari 2004) that the end of the Cold War would, contrary to the expectations of most, deliver new challenges, instead of the anticipated *Pax Americana*. Indeed, according to Huntington, the 'Velvet Curtain of culture' would replace the 'Iron Curtain' where a historical confrontation, expressed in military form, between the Christian and the Islamic civilizations, would take place. Huntington saw the relationship between Islam and 'Western culture' as solely conflictual since, according to him, Islam (and at a certain level of Confucianism) challenges the 'perfect' and progressive Greek-Judeo-Christian heritage on which all of the West has been founded.

Casanova (2011), in his analysis of the clash of civilizations theory, acknowledged that Huntington was a pioneer in understanding the increasing relevance that culture and world religion would have after the collapse of communist regimes:

He breaks with the secularism long hegemonic in the field of Realpolitik and inter-national relations by bringing religion to the centre of civilisational analysis and by insisting that the contemporary global condition facilitates the return of the old civilisations and world religions as significant cultural systems and as imagined communities, overlapping and at times in competition with the imagined community of the nation. (Casanova 2011: 8)

Yet, Huntington's views have attracted more criticism than praise within academia. One of the main criticisms (see Pippidi and Mindreuta 2002; Fox 2001; Casanova 2011) focuses on the monolithic understanding of both civilization in general and the idea of a unified Western culture. Indeed, Bulliet (2004), in his provocative *The Case for Islamo-Christian Civilization*, has suggested that if we carefully observe historical and cultural facts, we can notice that to speak, as Huntington does, of a Judeo-Christian civilization, as opposed to a Confucian-Islamic one, does not make sense. Other scholars, such as Gerges (1999), have noticed that if a clash were to exist, it would be a clash of interests rather than of civilizations. Kupchan (2002) has also highlighted that Huntington ignores the effect that colonialism had on Muslims and their economic and political disenfranchisement with dictatorial Middle Eastern governments, which were for a long time supported by the West, and how this has produced popular support for extremist Islamic movements.

Halliday (1996)[4] instead explains the high level of attention that the clash of civilizations theory has attracted. He suggests that the theory of a clash of civilizations offered the myth of a new challenge, a new battle against evil, which appealed to the imaginations of both politicians and the mass media. Casanova (2011: 9) agrees that Huntington has provided an essentialist view of culture, civilization and world religions, which are seen to possess 'some unchangeable core essence', but also correctly points out that the theory 'conceives of civilisations as territorially bounded geopolitical units akin to superpowers and nation-states' (2011: 9). Finally, Casanova thinks that Huntington presents an 'unabashed assertion of western global hegemony that can easily turn the prognosis of the clash of civilisations into a dangerous self-fulfilling prophecy' (2011: 9). Rather, Casanova points out, Huntington has not noticed the different effects that globalization has had on world religions. Indeed, on the one hand, globalization provides the greatest opportunity for 'old civilisations and world religions to free themselves from the straightjacket of the nation-state' (2011: 12), so as to regain the state of being a transnational cultural force they had been before the development of nation-states. However, at the same time, globalization can also represent a threat since, according to Casanova (2011: 12), 'globalisation threatens to dissolve the intrinsic link between sacred time, sacred space and sacred people common to all world religions, and with it the seemingly essential bonds between histories, peoples and territories which have defined all civilisations'. Yet, Turner has observed that Huntington's thesis cannot be fully understood if we do not consider its philosophical and sociological pedigree, which is dependent

> on an academic tradition of political philosophy that sought to define sovereignty in terms of civilisational struggles between friend and foe, namely the legacy of Carl Schmitt and Leo Strauss. It is not possible to

understand fully the contemporary 'state of emergency' and 'clash of civilisations' without a re-appraisal in particular of the political theology of Schmitt. While Jürgen Habermas (1989: 135) expressed the hope that the Anglo-Saxon world would escape contagion from the Schmittian revival, his optimism was probably premature. The attack on New York has made Schmitt's ideas about state emergency, the crisis of liberalism, 'decisionist politics' and the division between friend and foe highly relevant to understanding contemporary American politics. (2002: 2)

Huntington's thesis, however, found a supporter in Osama bin Laden, who, during an interview, stated:

> I say that there is no doubt about this. This [Clash of Civilisations] is a very clear matter, proven in the Qur'an and the traditions of the Prophet, and any true believer who claims to be faithful shouldn't doubt these truths, no matter what anybody says about them. What goes for us is whatever is found in the Book of God and the hadith of the Prophet. But the Jews and Americans have come up with a fairytale that they transmit to the Muslims, and they've unfortunately been followed by the local rulers [of the Muslims] and a lot of people who are close to them, by using 'world peace' as an excuse. That is a fairytale that has no substance whatsoever! (bin Laden, Lawrence and Howarth 2005: 124–5)

The rhetoric here is not as in the case of Bush, political, or as in the case of Huntington, academic, but rather theological: the clash of civilizations as a divine plan sanctioned in the Qur'an and Hadiths. As we have discussed, the discourse of civilization creates categories and, with them, classifications. Just as Bush declared on 20 September 2001 that 'the civilised world is rallying to America's side' (cited in Collet 2009: 469), implying that whoever, be it a nation, organization or a person, disagreed with the US War on Terror was uncivilized, bin Laden declared that 'real Muslims' should commit to jihad since, according to him, 'world peace' was just a fairytale created by the evil civilization, the Judeo-Christian West, to deprive Muslims of their only weapon: faith in jihad and, of course, in bin Laden's views of Islam as a religion. The clash of civilizations, then, moves from theory to practice.

Civilization, fears and common sense

We have discussed the political and scholarly idea of civilization and the impact that the so-called clash of civilizations theory has had on those fields.

Yet, often, very little is known about what ordinary people, both Muslims and non-Muslims, think of the issue/affair. Do the majority agree that there is a 'clash of civilizations' in action or, maybe, explain the current conflictual realties in a different way? If people perceive that a clash between the Christian West and the Muslim world exists, in what way do they frame/think of it? Although some of the answers will be provided in the rest of the book in greater detail and depth, studies have shown that the War on Terror and even recent events, such as the Arab Spring, have been read in the West in many instances as a confrontation between the so-called 'civilized' values of the West and 'un-civilized' values represented by Islam. Of course, in the case of Muslim communities and Islamic countries, the perception of such events is just the opposite. In conflict areas that see some Muslims resisting occupation or fighting dictatorial governments (e.g. Palestine, Afghanistan, Iraq, Chechnya and Pakistan), the idea of a clash of civilizations is very popular and widespread (Hafez 2003). People tend to perceive of such conflicts as a clash between good and evil, between the civilized and the barbaric and between holy resistance and satanic oppression (Bowden 2007) or between victims and terrorists. However, even in Western countries, surveys have shown that Muslims have perceived the so-called War on Terror as a conflict with Islam as a religion (McCauley and Stellar 2010).

For instance, most respondents of focus groups of Scottish Muslims who discussed 'civilisation' and the 'clash of civilisations' (Marranci 2007; 2009) agreed that civilizations do exist, such that one can indeed speak of an Islamic civilization – which they saw as superior in moral and ethical values to the Western one. All the respondents agreed on Western civilization as an expression of Christianity. The majority agreed that the West is corrupt and can corrupt Islam, that the West has lost its real Christian values (which was an interesting contradiction with the idea of the West as an expression of Christianity), and that the clash of civilizations is rather inevitable. For instance, Habib, a 24-year-old British Muslim of Bangladeshi heritage/origin, while discussing the concept of civilization, mentioned/said:

> I think that there are different civilisations. The Qur'an speaks of civilisations, it speaks of Rome and Romans, and the rise and fall of civilisation. So, I think that civilisations exist and our religion tells us that they are divided. There are the Christians, the Jews and the Muslims, then within these there are other divisions. Indeed, the Qur'an tells us that the human ummah is the only one which is divided, since the birds, for example, are a single ummah. I think that civilisations are either good or bad: they are good if they follow God, but if they reject God, they become bad and people will suffer. We have to try to avoid clashing, but we know that it is part of life – and civilisations, like humans, clash, but they clash over the problem of

the truth. Islam is under attack because it has the truth and the Western civilisation rejects it and wants to impose its Godless view of life and law. (quoted in Marranci 2009: 140)

Similarly, such sense of conflict and distrust is widely present in Western countries, where Muslims are often seen as a potential enemy or danger to the nation's cultural values. As several polls have shown, even years after 9/11, the distrust towards Muslims has not decreased. A Gallup poll in 2010 showed that 43 per cent of Americans had 'a little' prejudice against Muslims, while 53 per cent held an unfavourable view of Islam as a religion (Gallup News Service 2010). The situation is, unfortunately, not much better in the UK either. A poll conducted by BBC Radio 1 Newsbeat, on 25 September 2013, suggested that among the '1,000 young people questioned, 28% said Britain would be better off with fewer Muslims, while 44% said Muslims did not share the same values as the rest of the population. Some 60% thought the British public had a negative image of Muslims.' Only 48 per cent agreed that Islam is a peaceful religion.[5]

We can read 'not sharing the same values' as being synonymous with *not sharing the same civilization*; in other words, these British youth see Islam and Muslims as something external (and threatening) to the foundation and essence of what they imagine Western civilization to be. What brings so many people to directly or indirectly believe that a clash of civilizations exists? One of the most relevant processes that my research has identified (Marranci 2006, 2009) deals with what Bhabha (1994) identifies as a 'circle of panic'. To illustrate, Bhabha (2001) reports the story of the 'chapati mystery'. In 1856 across northern India, new rifles and new carriers for ammunition were provided to Muslim and Hindu soldiers of the East India Company. The ammunition was to be carried in a paper-wrapped cartridge which was waterproofed with some grease. To open the cartridge, a soldier had to use his teeth. In 1857, rumours among the soldiers spread that the grease used was a mixture of pork and cow fat (forbidden to Muslims and Hindus, respectively). The British tried to convince the soldiers that it was made from mutton, but they also feared that a rebellion was near. This was because they came to know that chapati bread was inexplicably being hand-delivered from village to village. The British thought that a secret message was transmitted through the chapatis. In reality nobody knew why those chapatis were being hand-delivered. Both these rumours – pork and cow fat in the cartridge, and secret messages in hand-delivered chapatis – facilitated the 1857 uprising.

Bhabha thus argues (2001: 332), 'What is the vertiginous chapati saying to me? The "indeterminate" circulation of meaning as rumour or conspiracy, with its perverse, psychic affects of panic constitutes the intersubjective realm of revolt and resistance.' The 'rumours' in our case are basically twofold – similar and yet opposite. On the one hand, an increasing number of Muslims imagine a monolithic 'West' that seeks to wipe out Islam and, consequently, Muslim identities. On the other, many non-Muslims increasingly imagine a monolithic Islam as a threat not just to security but to the very existence of Western civilization as they understand it.

I have observed (Marranci 2006) that 'rumours', in particular those suggesting a threat, increase fear through another process that can explain the chapati story as well. Bateson observed that in some cases, iterations among groups are 'characterised by interchanges of behaviour such as that the more A exhibited a given behaviour, the more B was likely to exhibit the same behaviour' (2002: 98). He defined such relations as 'symmetrical changes', and macro examples of these processes are, for instance, armament races. He identified also another form of complementary change, which is the intensification of dominate-subordinate relations. A characteristic of both changes is that they tend to show progressive escalation, which Bateson called 'schismogenesis'. He noticed that certain rituals or realities can either inhibit or stimulate schismogenic relations. As we shall see in this book, the 'circle of panic' and the associated 'rituals' are reinforcing the symmetrical schismogenic property of a clash of civilizers, of which the War on Terror is nothing but a product. Yet, each player is aiming to bring the opponent within a complementary schismogenesis.

For this reason, the circle of panic can be understood through the analysis that Bhabha (2001: 335–6) offers of the mysterious chapati:

> It is at the enunciative level that the humble chapati circulates both a panic of knowledge and power. The great spreading fear, more dangerous than anger, is equivocal, circulating wildly on both sides. It spreads beyond the knowledge of ethnic or cultural binarisms and becomes a new, hybrid space of cultural difference in the negotiation of colonial power-relations. Beyond the barracks and the bungalow opens up an antagonistic, ambiguous area of engagement that provides, in a perverse way, a common battleground.

The chapati this time is the fear that 'civilisation' is threatened, or as politicians tend to say 'our way of life', which, of course, is seen as morally superior to any other way of life. As Bhabha has suggested, even a humble symbol or idea may circulate 'both a panic of knowledge and power'. Such panic of knowledge and power is, in our case, expressed in the message, which the mass media, as we shall see, repeats and amplifies, that the civilized world is facing a war, albeit an anomalous one, where the conflict is not limited to the military field; rather, 'hearts and minds' are at stake. The minds (and hearts) referred to here are the minds of Muslims – Kepel (2004) captures this in his book, which is aptly titled *The War for Muslim Minds: Islam and the West*. On the other side of the conflict, bin Laden has prepared his own 'chapati' for the Muslim *ummah*. Repeated statements such as, 'They came to fight Islam and its people on the pretext of fighting terrorism'; 'I tell you that these events have split the entire world into two camps: one of faith, with no hypocrites, and one of unbelief' and 'Rather, the battle is between Muslims – the people of Islam – and the global Crusaders' (bin Laden, Lawrence and Howarth 2005: 105, 108), have helped bin Laden and al-Qaida to capitalize on the fears of some Muslims, both in the West and in the Muslim world, that Islam itself is in danger. The simplification, of course, was made even more believable by complex geopolitical conflicts in the Middle East and other Muslim countries, such as the Chechen conflict, the Iraq War and so forth.

A final important element of the strong appeal that the 'clash of civilizations' has, for both ordinary people and leaders, is its commonsensical essence. Indeed, common sense will have a very important role in our attempt to understand the increasingly tense relations between Muslims and non-Muslims. Philosophy, through thinkers such as Descartes, Vico, Shaftesbury, Thomas Reid and Kant, has paid attention to common sense and provided some interesting readings of it (see the critical review by Gadamer 1965). By contrast, the discipline of anthropology demonstrates a lack of attention to the concept. Geertz in this respect, as in others, offers a positive exception. Geertz (1975) has suggested that common sense 'is, in short, a cultural system, though not usually a very tightly integrated one, and it rests on the same basis that any other such system rests; the conviction by those whose possess it is of its value and validity' (1975: 8). Common sense, according to him, has some universal characteristics, which he defines as semi-qualities: naturalness, practicalness, thinness, immethodicalness and accessibleness. Naturalness can be identified as the most fundamental aspect since common sense 'represents matters – that is, certain matters and not others – as being what they are in the simple nature of the case' (1975: 18). Practicalness is a consequence of the former; 'for it is not "practicalness" in the narrowly pragmatical sense of the useful, but in the broader, folk-philosophical sense of sagacity that is involved' (1975: 20). Thinness, or literalness, is the characteristic of common sense to avoid any complex explanation, but rather to represent matters 'as being precisely what they seem to be, neither more nor less' (1975: 22). Geertz labelled common sense as also 'immethodicalness' since its 'wisdom is shamelessly and unapologetically ad hoc ... [it is a] potpourri of disparate notions ... which not only characterise systems of common sense generally, but which in fact recommend themes capable of grasping the vast multifariousness of life in the world' (1975: 24). Common sense does not deconstruct the observed reality, rather it explains it in the most efficient, parsimonious and selective way. Indeed, the last aspect of common sense that Geertz highlights is accessibleness, a natural consequence of the other aspects of common sense. Accessibleness, according to Geertz, 'is simply the assumption, in fact the insistence, that any person with faculties reasonably intact can grasp common sense conclusions and, indeed, once they are unequivocally enough stated, will not only grasp but embrace them' (1975: 24). It is interesting to note that some of the elements discussed about common sense can be considered to be also elements of 'stereotypes'.

It is not difficult for the reader to see how the discourse of 'civilizations', and the consequent idea of a clash of civilizations, is increasingly becoming commonsensical. The simplification in media reports, political discussion, fictional literature (Randall 2011) and, of course, Hollywood (Dixon 2004), facilitates a stereotyped reading of the aftermath of 9/11 and the War on Terror (Dimaggio 2008). The idea that a clash of civilizations is taking place has increased during recent years, as the discussion about the failure of multiculturalism in the UK and Germany may show (Cesari 2013; Kundnani 2012). In this case, politicians like Cameron and Merkel advocated the assimilation of, in particular, Muslims within a national system of values or, to put it differently, Western civilizational values. The idea is clear: either you are part of it or you are against it. The complexity, for instance, of Muslim migrations to the UK, or the economic and social realties in which most Muslims in the UK (and the rest of Europe) live (Marranci 2008), was completely ignored. The political discourse, and the debate that surrounded it, demonstrated how common sense directed the discussion, such as the naturalness, to use Geertz's terminology, of the concept of values, the practicalness of 'when in Rome, do as the Romans do', the thinness of the concept of democracy and freedom, immethodicalness concerning perceptions of Muslims in the country, and the accessibleness of the idea of 'us' versus 'them'. All such discourse provides the new idea of civilization with an aura of common sense that is as attractive as it is convincing.

Civilizational common sense, as we may call it, exists not only among white non-Muslim 'Westerners' but also among some Muslims and Muslim groups. In this case, the civilizational common sense focuses on the fact that, as we have seen, Islam is under attack, that all non-Muslims lack values and, in particular, a real sense of justice and morality. It is rather evident that the supposed clash of civilizations is expressed through a clash of common sense between similar, parallel yet opposite, ways of thinking that in both cases remain more often than not a 'pensée unique'.

Conclusion

Civilization: a concept with a complex history and a new revival in the aftermath of 9/11 and the War on Terror. Today, more than ever, belief in the clash of civilizations affects not only macro and geopolitical decisions, but also governments' internal policies in areas such as security, immigration and, in particular, multiculturalism. Huntington, in reality, has not put forth a theory, but rather expressed in a theoretical form what ordinary people (Muslims and non-Muslims alike) saw as common sense. The idea of 'culture' as an ontology, and religion as the ultimate expression of it, existed before 9/11, of course. Yet, the terrorist attack reinforced such general essentialization, and perceptions about Islam as a danger to western liberties and 'lifestyle' became increasingly commonsensical among some sections of the population. The political rhetoric is a result of such reality, rather than, as some have suggested, the cause (Kumar 2012).

Some Muslims and non-Muslims living in Western countries look at each other through the prism of their own respective civilizational values. The fear that the other 'group' has the power to dilute, threaten or alienate one's own 'values' reinforces a circle of panic that is marked by a schismogenic property (Marranci 2006). Yet, it is not only the circle of panic that is schismogenic; the desired solution, as we see in this book, of those actively involved in what they see as a clash of civilizations, is subject to the same dynamic. While the circle of panic is expressed through symmetrical schismogenesis, the aim of what I call 'civilisers' is to impose a complementary schismogenesis upon the other: a relationship of dominance-submission.

The struggle between 'civilisers' is not only taking place on the battlefield, in the rooms of command, in suicide actions, through the murder of innocents or attacks on 'soft targets', or, by contrast, through incredibly sophisticated technologies such as 'predator drones', but also in the more difficult-to-observe, everyday lives and decisions, and also in attempts to reject or impose 'culture', 'world views', 'values' and 'life styles' which are seen as incompatible. The War on Terror, its rhetoric and its paraphernalia has hidden this more complex, and dangerous, reality of civilizational discourse, and with it the clash of civilizers.

Notes

1   CNN, 9 November 2001, "Bush: 'We wage a war to save civilization itself'" http://edition.cnn.com/2001/US/11/08/rec.bush.speech/index. html?iref=allsearch.

2 Cited in Collet (2009: 458).

3 Cited in Collet (2009: 462).

4 See also Seib (2004) and Faoud (1993).

5 BBC Newsbeat, 25 September 2013, 'Quarter of young British people "do not trust Muslims"' http://www.bbc.co.uk/newsbeat/24204742 (accessed 25 September 2013).

3

Labels, stigmas and ethos

It was in one of those eternal summers of Singapore that Raziq,[1] while sharing a very sweet *teh tarik*,[2] asked me if I thought, as an anthropologist, whether Islam was compatible with Western liberal democracy and how Muslims in the West cope in a place where their religion can be attacked and denigrated as happened with Salman Rushdie's *Satanic Verses* (1998) and more recently with the Danish Cartoons affair. The question is not surprising if one is familiar with the strong enforcement of 'religious harmony' and the 'hard' multiculturalism in Singapore (Marranci 2011; Chua 2003; Goh 2010) or the repression of any controversial comment or joke about Islam in neighbouring Malaysia, where several bloggers had been arrested.[3] The idea that Islam as a religion and way of life is incompatible with Western democracy is certainly not a new one, as we have seen in the previous chapter. Yet, surely in the aftermath of 9/11 and the start of the War on Terror, such discussions have spread from academic environments to the general population, through the mass media and the uncountable number of editorials, as well as through Youtube videos and personal blogs.

We cannot study one aspect – that is, how some Muslims react to the secularism/democracy debate, of which freedom of speech is central, as the Charlie Hebdo shooting has shown – without observing and studying the other – how the War on Terror and its rhetoric has reinforced the idea of a total freedom of speech and a strong secularist perception of it. Indeed, what this chapter will show is that the process *is* schismogenic and involves a very key concept: the concept of *ethos*. To fully understand how the civilizers on both sides of the battlefield act, we need to discuss the power of labels used by both non-Muslims and Muslims to create stigma, which is useful to impose, internally upon the in-group but also against the out-group, that ethos which defines 'who is human'.

Indeed, Raziq, even before I could provide my answer, stated: 'Today many Muslims follow "liberal Islam", even here in Singapore and even when they do not call themselves liberals. They for example say that *hadd*[4] penalties should be suspended or even abolished – even in Islamic countries; they suggest that western democracy is equivalent to *shura*,[5] they believe in freedom of speech without restraint. I think this is liberal Islam and the war on terror and the invasion of Muslim countries have started to change Islam.' Raziq was not just a Malay member of the Singaporean Muslim community, but an *asatizah*, an Islamic teacher, from the respectable organization PERGAS.[6] A considerable portion of the Muslim population in the world, including the secularly educated, considers the War on Terror as both an ideological and physical war against 'orthodox' Islam; in other words, a war to make Islam a religion compatible not only with the European Enlightenment, but also with capitalism. On the other side of the spectrum, many non-Muslims living in Western countries suggest exactly the opposite: that liberal democracy and the Western way of life, in particular, freedom of speech, are threatened by an increasing Muslim presence because, according to them, Islam is incompatible with the West (Spruyt 2007). Much of the anthropological (but also sociological and political) literature has focused on one or the other sides of the discourse when instead it is important to see this as one discourse, which is the result of a dynamic, albeit conflictual. Before we do so, we need to have a brief idea of the academic discourse focusing on Islam and concepts such as democracy, secularism and, in general, political Islam. I have engaged elsewhere in the debate concerning what some define as 'fundamentalist Islam' (Marranci 2009), so I wish here to provide only some 'paradigmatic' views of what I tend to see as a problematic approach to the understanding of Muslims as social political actors.

How have anthropologists discussed Muslims and their political identities?

Anthropologists of the colonial era conducted fieldwork and studied in regions where the majority practised Islam, but they did not study them as Muslims, rather as part of tribes and ethnic groups; these scholars saw religion as an institution and as a secondary factor in the lives of their informants (Marranci 2008; Gilsenan 1990). E. E. Evans-Pritchard remains a noteworthy exception with his study of the Sanusiyya Sufi order in Libya (Evans-Pritchard 1949) since 'the originality of Evans-Pritchard's book was to show how a specifically Muslim institution – the Sufi order – could be established along extensive trans-Saharan trade routes and subsequently used to mobilize "tribal" groups against the Italian occupation of Libya' (Soares and Osella 2009: 53). We would need to wait until the middle of the 1960s to see a new attempt to bring Islam back within the anthropological analysis of North African and Middle Eastern societies. As I have discussed elsewhere (Marranci 2008: 34–47), Gellner first (1963, 1968, 1969 and 1981) and Geertz just after (1968) have provided not only the first systematic attempts to understand Islam as a social force shaping Muslim communities but also an analysis of the political dimensions of Islam in Muslim societies. The two scholars disagreed about the role that Islam has in the shape of Muslim societies; for Gellner, Islam is nothing less than 'a blue print for social order' (1981: 1), while Geertz viewed Islam as providing 'frames of perception' as well as 'blueprints for conduct' (Geertz 1968: 68). Both anthropologists agreed that Islam challenges secularism.

For Gellner, Islam is mainly a scripturalist religion which demonstrates ideological elements conducive towards fundamentalism, since it claims not only to be the perfect and final religion (something, of course, not uncommon for religions), but also that there is no room for new prophets because Muslims consider Muhammad as the seal of the prophets. Adding to these theological aspects, Gellner has pointed out two other structural aspects: first of all, Islam has no clergy, and therefore no religious hierarchy, like for instance Christianity has, and secondly, no political authority can claim power over Islam because, according to Gellner, it does not 'equate faith with the beliefs of any community or society. ... But the trans-social truth which can sit in judgment on the social is a Book' (1981: 101). The Book (i.e. the Qur'an) is the ultimate authority of 'rapidly successful conquerors *who soon were state*' (Gellner 1981: 100, author's emphasis). Gellner's views of Islam are monolithic and Islam is not expected to change other than perhaps in certain reforms to make space for modernity (Soares and Osella 2009: 52) in a selective way.[7] Certainly the reader may not be surprised to find that Gellner has categorically concluded that Muslims 'could have democracy, or secularism, but not both' (1981: 60). In other words, if Muslim societies have democracy, they would inevitably see secularism eroded in favour of an increasingly sharia-based state; by contrast, only a dictatorship can impose a secular model of society because it can manipulate and control, and so limit, the role and influence of Islam within society.

Geertz's main reading of Islam can be found in *Islam Observed* (1968). I have discussed elsewhere the relevance of this work for the anthropology of Islam (Marranci 2008), so here I wish to focus on his understanding of the relation between Islam, modernity and political Islam. If Gellner saw Islam as anti-democratic but not anti-modern, for Geertz, the potential fundamentalist nature of Islam can be traced to the tension between common sense, faith and modernity. At the centre of his argument, culture, ethos and social order have a strong relevance. For instance, Geertz has noticed 'the conviction that values one holds are grounded in the inherent structure of reality, that between the way one ought to live and the way things really are there is an unbreakable inner connection' (Geertz 1968: 97). Such connections are, of course, mediated through symbols, in our case, the religious symbols which 'render the world view believable and the ethos justifiable and they do it by involving each in support of the other' (ibid.). Geertz, in his book, through a comparative approach observed two different societies, Morocco and Indonesia, which, however, have a parallel experience in moving from an esoteric, saint-based reading of the Qur'an to a scripturalist reading of it. It is this phase of the two societies' transformation that is more salient for us. Indeed, Geertz has suggested that the establishment of Western colonialism and domination created a crisis through the rapid social change it brought. The answer to the crisis was the re-discovery of the sacred scripture, instead of the charismatic saint-leader, who was seen now as representative of 'tradition'. Indeed, according to Geertz, the scripturalist phase was an answer to 'the industrial revolution, Western intrusion and domination, the decline of the aristocratic principle of government, and the triumph of radical nationalism' (1968: 57). This, he has explained, created a paradox in which Islam became the 'justification for modernity without itself actually becoming modern' (1968: 69). Political Islam, or what Geertz has labelled as fundamentalism, is a reaction to modernity, with the latter being – Soares and Osella noticed both Geertz and Gellner making this point – 'a Western prerogative that spreads with colonialism. While it might be taken up or contested, it will invariably lead to problematic outcomes, such as fledgeling states that have failed to transform themselves into fully modern functioning polities' (2009: 53–4).

Soares and Osella suggest that 'shortcomings notwithstanding, Gellner and Geertz both pointed to the importance of religion in societies undergoing profound social transformations' (2009: 54). Yet, they seem to forget that such models would become the main paradigm through which Islam as a sociopolitical force would be presented within the 'civilising' discourse. Indeed, it is undeniable that both Gellner and Geertz, with their Weberian (Weber 2002) assumption of modernity as a Western product exported through colonialism, adhere to Huntington's same perception of cultures/ religions as civilizations. Authors such as Bernard Lewis (2003) or even pundits such as Robert Spencer (2005 and 2007), Daniel Pipes (2002) and, of course, Bat Ye'or (2002 and 2004) provide just a caricature of the above model: 'Muslim society' (in the singular for Gellner) is defined by Islam and, of course, fundamentalism is part of the genome of such religion. I (Marranci 2006, 2008 and 2009) among several others (see for instance Varisco 2005; Esposito 1999 and in particular Mamdani 2004) have provided criticism of such monolithic views of Islam and the essentialist view that Muslims are just that, Muslims, a product of 'culture talk' (Mamdani 2004), rather than humans with different beliefs and acting in multiple contexts.

More recent works have attempted to explain the interconnection between politics and Islam, and Eickelman and Piscatori, focusing on what they call 'Muslim politics', have argued that Muslims today objectify their own religion, developing heightened self-consciences of Islam as a religious system (2004: 63):

> Objectified understanding of Islamic beliefs and practices have irrevocably transformed Muslim relations to sacred authority. Of critical importance in this process has been a 'democratisation' of the political process of Islam and the development of a standardised language, inculcated by mass higher education, the mass media, travel and labor migration.

As in the case of Geertz and Gellner, the anthropologist Eickelman and the political scientist Piscatori seem to represent Muslims as passive in the formation of their beliefs: their religion is 'inculcated' through the toll of modernity. Furthermore, Soares and Osella correctly argue that 'Eickelman and Piscatori's analytical turn placed contemporary Muslim politics within epistemological shifts and social processes ... ordinarily associated in mainstream social theory with Western modernity' (2009: 4). In conclusion, Eickelman and Piscatori advance the idea that inevitably Muslims will be absorbed within the liberal system and Muslim politics normalized as just one of the many 'politics'. Of course, as Soares and Osella suggest, this is not the only way to understand the relation between Muslims, politics and modernity. Several anthropologists have challenged the Weberian idea of modernity as the epitome of Western civilization and as something that is seen only in it; they have, in fact, identified alternative modernities in Muslim societies (see for instance Brenner 1996; Göle 2002; White 2011; Mahmood 2011).

Antoun, however, has suggested that 'the fundamentalist's protest and outrage is against the ideology of modernism. ... [Its] protest is also against the secular nation-state, which it regards as instrumental in pushing religion to margins' (2001: 153–4). He has also argued that the scripturalism identified by Geertz is in reality a psychological tool to provide a sense of security and certainty through the authority of the text, since through the sacred text even negative realities can be turned into positive events that are inspirational for the 'truth' believer. I have expressed my concerns (2009: 60–65) about Antoun's views on the definition of a fundamentalist, since his article 'The Prophet's Way: Conversations with a Muslim Fundamentalist' (2001: 133–51) seems to suggest that any pious Muslim is in reality a fundamentalist or the simple acts of devotion that are rather common in many mainstream mosques are in reality to be read as fundamentalism and, as such, anti-modern. Mahmood's study of Muslim women shows that such a clear-cut definition cannot be assumed; for instance she noticed that, 'the piety activists seek to imbue each of the various spheres of contemporary life with a regulative sensibility that takes its cue from the Islamic theological corpus rather than from modern secular ethics' (2011: 47). What for Antoun would be clear evidence of fundamentalism is an alternative system of ethos for Mahmood.

Another common approach, which attempts to suggest that Islam per se is not a problem but rather the political discourse of Muslims is, follows a different rationale. For example, Noorani (2002) and Esposito (1991 and 1999) suggest that, contrary to what Huntington or Lewis may think, there is nothing wrong with Islam as a religion. Rather the issue is what Noorani identifies as a fundamentalist impostor who 'has misused a noble faith as a political weapon. Of course, Islam does have a political vision; but it is far removed from the Islam which very many Muslims and most non-Muslims imagine it to be' (Noorani 2002: ix). Esposito, instead, has suggested that some Muslims manipulate Islam as a political tool to change their societies or oppose 'imperialism', and this makes them unable to interpret their religion correctly, because their interpretation is corrupted by the irresistible temptation that human beings have to manipulate religion for the sake of political and nationalistic goals. Noorani goes further in his argument than Esposito, since at the end of it, he suggests that Muslims with radical ideas are nothing other than Muslims without Islam.

The debate is not only about modernity and democracy and rejections of those by some Muslims. Another central theme is essential to the debate, even more so after 9/11 and the War on Terror: secularism. Talal Asad has surely provided the most influential anthropological study of secularism in his *Formations of the Secular* (Asad 2003), about which Bangstad (2009: 188) has pointed out that 'if, as Varisco (2007: 9) claims, it became a kind of initiatory bismillah to cite Edward Said in literary texts about colonial discourse, the same can be said with regard to citing Asad in anthropological texts on secularism – or, for that matter, in anthropological texts on Islam'. Asad has stated that secularism goes beyond the commonsensical separation of religion from state institutions, since

'the secular' should not be thought of as the space in which *real* human life gradually emancipates itself from the controlling power of 'religion' and thus achieves the latter's relocation. It is this assumption that allows us to think of religion as 'infecting' the secular domain or as replicating within it the structure of theological concepts. The concept of the secular today is part of a doctrine called secularism. Secularism doesn't simply insist that religious practice and belief be confined to a space where they cannot threaten political stability or the liberties of the 'free-thinking' citizens. Secularism builds on a particular conception of the world ('natural' and 'social') and of the problems generated by that world. (2003: 181, author's emphasis)

The 'secular', according to Asad, is a historical process formed through different concepts, practices and sensibilities, conceptually preceding the

political doctrine of secularism, and it cannot be understood as th
successor of 'religion' but rather as 'a category with a multi-layere
related to major premises of modernity' (Asad 2003: 278). Yet, why
process started and for what reason? For Asad, European history is cel
how 'the doctrine of secularism has been conceived and implemented i ...ie
rest of the modernising world' (Asad 2003: 25). Bangstad, in his thoughtful,
critical review of Asad's work on secularism, has rightly highlighted that 'the
binary between the "West" and the "non-West" is of course central to much
post-colonial theorising, and Asad is no exception in this regard' (Bangstad
2009: 192). As Bangstad (2009) noticed, Asad's work had a strong influence
on other studies such as those of Mahmood (2006 and 2011), in which the
binary categorization – 'West' and 'non-West' – continued. Silverstein (2003)
has agreed, for instance, with Mahmood's views that to apply a Western
liberal model of selfhood such as individualistic autonomy to Muslims and
their practices is probably inappropriate, but he has reminded us of another,
opposite, danger 'to equivocate on the degree of alterity to be ascribed
to "non-Western" (including on this account Islamic) traditions vis- a-vis
"Western" ones' (Silverstein 2003: 499).

Soares and Osella (2009: 55–7) have pointed out how anthropologists
such as Hefner (2000) observed that the flourishing of civil society within
Muslim majority countries, such as Indonesia, produced, what Hefner
called, 'civil Islam', and how 'civil Islam' is fully compatible with democracy,
democratic institutions and pluralism, since, although being able to influence
the government, activists do not aim to impose sharia or Islamicize the state.
Other authors, such as Olivier Roy (2006 and 2013) and Gilles Kepel (2004),
have affirmed that instead of aiming to Islamicize societies, certain Muslim
groups rather aim to Islamicize individuals; he explains this in the following
words:

> The forms of religiosity in Islam today are more or less the same as those
> found in Catholicism, Protestantism, and even Judaism. Contemporary
> adherents insist more on personal faith and individual spiritual experience.
> Such 'born again' believers rebuild their identities from the perspective
> of their rediscovery of religion. ... Today's Islamic revival shares the
> dogmatism, communitarism, and scripturalism of American evangelist
> movements: both reject culture, philosophy and even theology in favour of
> a literalist reading of the sacred texts and an immediate understanding of
> truth through individual faith. (Roy 2013: 18)

However, Soares and Osella seem to be sceptical of such changes and
suggest that 'scholars such as Roy and Kepel fail to take seriously modes and
spaces of political action beyond the purview of formal politics and the state'

(2009: 10). Rather, Soares and Osella suggest that there is a better way to understand Muslims in a changing world in which concepts such as 'modern' and 'secularism' have increasingly come to play a role in what Soares and Otayek have called *islam mondain*. (2007: 17). *Islam mondain*, explain the two scholars,

> points to ways of being Muslim that exist in secular societies and spheres, without necessarily being secular. ... *Islam mondain* is also a moral and moralizing Islam. However, it does not necessarily replace that of political Islam and does not in any way call into question the scholarly attention devoted to the latter; but it raises new questions because it seems to capture more adequately many Muslims' ways of being in the contemporary world. Those Muslims inhabiting this *islam mondain* might focus on self-improvement, the correct practice of Islam, and not just politics or the political, though they might attend to the latter as well. (Soares and Otayek 2007: 17, italics in the text)

Islam mondain, according to Soares and Otayek, attempts to distance itself from the Foucauldian model which some scholars (such Mahmood 2011; Hirschkind 2006), in their recent studies of piety movements, adopt.

Scripturalism; fundamentalism; piety movements; *islam mondain;* Islam as a blueprint for social order, or, on the contrary, as a blueprint for conduct; Islam as truth; Islam betrayed by manipulative impostors – all these are different topics, yet the main 'actor' in most of the literature, past and present, on these topics remains Islam. Furthermore, a meta-analysis of the available academic work on Islam/Muslims and democracy/secularism as well as political activism demonstrates that, as mentioned at the start of this chapter, the data and derived discussion is normally focused only on Islam and Muslims (and more on the former), and thus, the dynamics of interaction with non-Muslim environments, or what we may, using a term fashionable in the 1960s (Umpleby 1997), define as the *cybernetic space* between Islam and non-Islam and Muslim and non-Muslim, are missed.

Contexts, relations, dynamics, dialogue or diatribes which clearly exist in everyday interactions, in person as in cyberspace, include not only the conceptual categories of Islam and Muslim but also the inevitable ones of non-Muslim and non-Islam. Yet, surprisingly, from Gellner passing through Geertz, to more recent anthropologists such as Antoun, and even *islam mondain,* the cybernetic space that I mentioned above is forgotten, silenced as often it is in the fieldwork of the scholars. It is not difficult to understand the reasons for such relevant *omissis*. Despite the efforts within anthropology and sociology to avoid the essentialization of Muslims, evidence still suggests that what I have called 'the fallacy of the "Muslim mind theory"' (Marranci 2008: 6) remains, latently or explicitly, detectable, sometimes even in titles or subtitles, as in Kepel's book 'The war for Muslim minds' (2004).[8] This fallacy argues that it is religion that induces Muslims to believe, behave, act, think, argue and develop their identity *as Muslims* and not their disparate heritages, ethnicities, nationalities, experiences, gender, sexual orientations and, last but not least, minds.

Values, fears and ontologies

As we have observed above, the discussion and focus concerning Muslims and politics (understood in its wider meaning) concentrate on three main variables: modernity, secularism and democracy; or better the lack of it. Not only do many scholars working in Western academia assume often implicitly or explicitly the existence of a 'Muslim mind', but also they present the reality in dichotomic synecdoche: modernism/scripturalism, secularism/fundamentalism, democracy/sharia. These are not only dichotomies but are also indeed synecdoche, since, reduced to their label-function, such oppositions are derived by 'selecting' the parts of a much more complex system and set of traditions. The abstraction is such that history, geography and economic class disappear from the equation. Such a way of discussing Muslims as political actors derives from the same synecdochical representation of European history. For instance Almond, Appleby and Sivan, one of the most influential scholars on fundamentalism, has noticed,

> This is not the first time that Enlightenment expectations have been rebuffed by history. The ideas leading up to the rationalism of the French Revolution were succeeded by the clerico-conservative and authoritarian ideologies of the end of the eighteenth and the first part of nineteenth centuries. ... What we call fundamentalism is the third rebuff that history has administrated to 'modernization' and secularization since the eighteenth century. ... What is remarkable about the third rebuff is that it is being administrated after the great scientific revolutions of the twentieth century. (2003: 5)

There are some simple observations to advance here: the first is that the author presents European (i.e. Western) history as unilinear and progressive, rooted in European historical events and their consequences. Secondly, Enlightenment is presented as a civilizational 'Big Bang'. Yet, what we call Enlightenment, secularism or even modernism are the result of long and often bloody historical events (including the longest religious war recorded) which have never been unitary. Enlightenment in Spain and Italy or Greece had a very different development and is still understood in different ways than in the French, English or American contexts. I have called this kind of approach 'Eurocentric historical evolutionarism' (Marranci 2009).

Even the neologism *islam mondain*, which focuses on the interaction of Muslims with secular societies, particularly the West, and on secular practice, instead of treating Islam as a political ideology, shows great limitations. The term wants to indicate an assimilation of Muslims to the mainstream modern/ secular process by phenomenologically ordinary process. In other words, *islam mondain* seems to remove the theoretical problem by ignoring what Muslims say and focusing on what Muslims do within their secular societies. Although it is true that Muslims living in secular societies engage with, to quote Asad, the secular, this does not mean that they accept secularism or some fundamentals of our liberal democratic system. Quite the opposite, the reaction against 'secularism' is evident among substantial numbers of Muslims even when they live in Western liberal democracies. One of the best examples of this is in the attitudes that a very substantial number of Muslims have towards freedom of speech. At the same time, we can observe how freedom of speech is used to reinforce the civilizational discourse in which Islam is incompatible with the 'West' because of lacking the historical experience of the Enlightenment, the inevitable conclusion being that the only thing a Muslim can do is to assimilate, or, if I can say so, to be 'enlightened'. Part of that process is to reject their anti-modern ethos, clearly due, as we have seen, to faith in the scripture, and accept, as part of the new enlightened ethos, the denigration of their own religion, values and world views.

From the time of publication of *The Satanic Verses*, the question of whether Islam is a threat to freedom of speech has been expressed and debated. Incident after incident, many of them violent, shocked Western countries, which could not make sense of the reaction in the context of the twenty-first century. Muslims in many countries worldwide decided to protest. Such transnational and global attacks on 'Enlightenment values' such as freedom of speech saw the involvement of young, second- and even third-generation Muslims living in Western countries, which was perceived as the final evidence that Muslims could not be integrated, and that multiculturalism had failed. Although in the case of *The Satanic Verses*, the controversy derived more from the artistic decisions of the author than from an attempt to provoke Muslims or condemn Islam, such a precedent (the publication of such a book) inspired others to 'test' Muslims through direct criticism of Islam as a religion. A series of controversial works, often offensive to the sensitivity of Muslims worldwide, would thereafter appear from time to time, increasing the schismogenesis.

The site of controversy moved from the pages of a book to the high resolution of a short film. *Submission* aimed at sensitizing the audience to what Theo van Gogh, inspired by the controversial Ayaan Hirsi Ali, saw as the oppressive treatment of women in Islam. Yet, the printed verses of the Qur'an on the body of a half-naked woman reignited the anger of Muslims globally. This time van Gogh became the secular martyr of freedom of speech and thought. Dutch Moroccan Mohammed Bouyeri brutally slaughtered the film-maker and pinned a letter on Van Gogh's body with a knife that threatened Hirsi Ali and promised more blood on Dutch streets and the ultimate damnation of the Netherlands. Drastic protection had to be organized for Hirsi Ali.

Just a year later, twelve disrespectful caricatures of Muhammad created a new wave of violent protests among Muslims that was followed by familiar claims about the incompatibility of Islam and Muslims with Enlightened tolerant Europe. Flemming Rose, culture editor of the Danish newspaper Jyllands-Posten, commissioned the cartoons which were printed on 30 September 2005. The protests caused 'hundreds of deaths, burning embassies, a massive boycott of Danish and Norwegian products in the Muslim world, and severe repercussions against media staff across the world, where newspapers chose to republish the cartoons in whole or part. In Denmark, there were several death threats against the illustrators and Flemming Rose himself' (Lindekilde, Mouritsen and Zapata-Barrero 2009).

Meanwhile in the Netherlands, after Volkert van der Graaf assassinated Pim Fortuyn in 2002, Dutch MP Geert Wilders produced the YouTube film *Fitna* in March 2008 that aimed to show what he considers to be the Islamization of Europe and the danger of Islam, which according to him is a political ideology similar to Nazism, rather than a religion. Geert Wilders, in fact, has compared the Qur'an to Hitler's *Mein Kampf*, and as such something to be subjected to the same state ban. Of course, this has highly offended Muslims who have reacted in different ways. Geert Wilders had to defend his views in court, where they were acknowledged as part of his freedom of speech and not discriminatory against Muslims per se. Some years later another film, this time produced in the United States by an Egyptian Copt, *Innocence of Muslims*, of which a trailer in Arabic was released in September 2012 on YouTube, sparked new violent international protests, with over 50 deaths including that of US Ambassador in Libya, J. Christopher Stevens. Cities such as Sydney, totally unconnected to the event, witnessed self-organized – through Twitter and Facebook – violent protests (Roose 2013).

If Muslims see these accidents as a provocation and direct attack on Islam, its value system as well as Muslims as believers, some academics and politicians, particularly in Europe and Australia, have responded to the Muslim reaction in very different ways. Some accused multiculturalism for the tolerance of intolerants, others suggested that Western governments were far too passive, and some went so far, as the Arabist Hans Jansen, to declare the risk of 'self-Islamization' (quoted in Spruyt 2007: 324). The idea that the 'West', understood as a civilizational entity, has lost not only its glorious past but even the capacity of defending its own values is a recurrent theme. Freedom of speech has become, in the rhetoric of most liberal Europeans, a 'Maginot line' to preserve the ethos of European (i.e. Western) Enlightenment. During a recent conference in Sydney, a professor in political science expressed this same idea:

> Islam today is not the Islam of the Ottoman Empire. Islam today is a globalised ideology. There are Muslims whom surely appreciate freedom of speech, for instance, but these are a tiny minority, often perceived as 'hypocrites' by their own. The majority follow Islam as an ideology and that ideology is the opposite of our modern values. Yet we let such values be eroded by both fear and a misled commitment to the wrong kind of tolerance.

Spruyt has expressed, in different words, the same concept: 'Out of fear for Muslim indignation about certain things, a society succumbs in advance to expected demands of respect and is even willing to at least temporarily put aside its own values' (Spruyt 2007: 324). It is important here to notice that Spruyt, similarly to the political scientist I met at the recent conference, is critical also about liberal ideas which are accused of being responsible for such a weak 'West'. The proposed solution is to reclaim what we can call the 'ethos' of Western civilization. Spruyt explains this in clear terms:

> A return to 'a quiet and becoming pride' of Western civilization and a restoration not only of a specific tradition in an impressive past, but an ideal that focused on classical, pre-modern virtues (like prudence, decency, and that liberty which is not license) and that cherishes these virtues as necessary antidote against the ideals of modernity, and needs constant cultivation. Loss of this pride is at the bottom of the lack of resistance to nihilism. A return to this ideal would lead to a becoming defence of Western tradition as defined by the traditions of Jerusalem, Athens, and Rome. The pillars of Western civilization would have to be self-consciously cherished, and this implies recognising the utmost importance of institutions that transmit the virtues of this civilization: families, religion, and education. Coherence and the cultural foundations of liberal democracy and the free market would be restored by implementing what Plato called agraphoi nomoi, unwritten laws: the bonds that hold together the social framework of a nation. (Spruyt 2007: 328)

What Spruyt, together with a few other activists, has openly expressed is what others say only in strict confidence or express only from behind the anonymous screen of a computer online. However, the perception that the West is at its most decadent point – also perceived as a decadence of the white race as Bonnett has suggested (2004: 36) – is parallel to the perception that some Muslims have of their own religion: the moral decadence of 'real' Islam because of Muslims' behaviour and Westernization.

Muslims are not Muslims anymore. 'You see, doc', said Farid, 'look us here in Singapore; sure we have shari'a courts for marriages, and yes, we may marry four wives, but in reality our life is immoral in many ways. We do not respect Islam. We are becoming like Christians not because we believe that Isa [i.e. Jesus] is the son of God,[9] but because we accept all these liberal ideas.' The term 'liberal' would be repeated again and again by my informants regardless of where they may live – in Europe or Southeast Asia. Facebook campaigns, through groups or personal posts, are developed to 'fight liberal Islam'. Freedom of speech, many think, is one of the main problems that Muslims face, and, of course, liberal Muslims, according to their contenders, try to justify even films like *Submission.* 'They are not real Muslims,' stated Umar, 'they are in love with the West and reject shari'a. The worst of all is Tariq Ramadan. He plays the pious Muslim but in reality we know he rejects even the implementation of shar'ia.'

Are these Muslims, who through global platforms such as the Internet (Bunt 2009), reinforce their perception of Islam as anti-liberal and anti-Western, the Sayyid Qutbs of our times? From a certain viewpoint, the positions expressed by Umar or Farid may remind us of Qutb's cultural shock during his time in the United States. Musallam (2005: 114) reports his reaction:

From Denver, Qutb writes that during his first year in the 'workshop' of 'the New World' ... he did not see, except in rare moments, a human face with a look that radiated the meaning of humanity. Instead, Qutb writes, he found harried crowds (jumu' rakidah) resembling an excited herd (qati' ha'ij) that knew only lust and money. He describes love (al-hubb) in America as merely a body that lusts after another body, or hungry animal aspirations, or even the flirtation (al-ghazal) that normally precedes 'the final step'. He adds that nature had bestowed on America many blessings, including natural and human beauty, but no one understood or felt this beauty except as animals and beasts.

The same moral indignation can be easily read in hundreds of ordinary conversations among Muslim friends posted on Facebook and other forums – these Muslims who often are considered by scholars to be the silent majority. Indeed, although such a majority would not resort to violence, unlike the very tiny minority who rioted over the Youtube film '*The Innocence of Muslims*', they still share with the minority the 'moral indignation' against, in some cases, the very West in which they were born, as in the case of the second and third generations living in Western nations.

What we can observe here is similarity in difference. It is my contention that although opposing each other, those who see the West as a decadent civilization threatened from within by the loss of virtues of the past and from outside by an illiberal and totalitarian Islam, and those individuals who happen to be Muslims and who see Islam as made decadent by a weak *ummah* which has lost adherence to sharia, and as affected by the immoral Christian West, have the same aim: to control and define the ethos of their groups and then to define 'who is human' – through the redefined ethos – in a universalistic perspective.

The clash of ethos

The rhetoric of contemporary civilizers, no different from their progenitors, is centred in the discourse of 'ethos' – that is, ideals, values and perceptions of how one ought to live. Ethos is a concept that is difficult to define. In English it has lost, as Reynolds (1993) has noticed, its deep Greek meaning, which, in our case, is very relevant. As Michael Halloran had observed,

> In contrast to modern notions of the person or self, *ethos* emphasises the conventional rather than the idiosyncratic, the public rather than the private. The most concrete meaning for the term in the Greek lexicon is 'a habitual gathering place', and I suspect that it is upon this image of people gathering together in a public place, sharing experiences and ideas, that its meaning as character rests. To have *ethos* is to manifest the virtues most valued by the culture to and for which one speaks. (in Reynolds 1993: 328)

Ethos, in this classic meaning, reveals a deep connection with habit, customs and values. It is to this deep meaning that the anthropologist Geertz refers as well: 'Ethos is made intellectually reasonable by being shown to represent a way of life implied by the actual state of affairs which the world-view describes and the world-view is made emotionally acceptable by being presented as an image of an actual state of affair of which such a way of life is an authentic expression' (1957: 422). Geertz advances the idea that ethos and worldviews are connected since 'between ethos and world-views, between the approved style of life and the assumed structure of reality, there is conceived to be a simple and fundamental congruence such that they complete one another and lend one another meaning' (1957: 424). As the anthropologist has also pointed out, such congruence provides 'an appearance of objectivity' so that, for instance in the case of myths, 'values are portrayed not as subjective human preferences but as the imposed conditions for life implicit in a world with a particular structure' (1957: 426–7).

When we analyse the 'Muslim conspiracy theory' (Fekete 2012), which inspired Anders Behring Breivik in his Oslo massacre, and much of the Muslims' conspiracy theories concerning the War on Terror, the similarities are startling. Breivik declared to be part of a mysterious organization called Knights Templar Europe of which he was AB Justiciar Knight Commander, cell 8. As Fekete correctly argues, Breivik's ideology is in reality shared by many in the mainstream political arena and with some observable results: debates about Muslim dress style, such as the burqa, the attempt to ban minarets from mosques (which was successful in Switzerland) and various 'self-defense' leagues, such as the English Defense League (EDL) or Stop Islamisation of Europe (SIOE) and Stop Islamization of America (SIOA), which are guided by charismatic leaders such as Pamela Geller and Robert Spencer and have millions of followers and supporters.

To an attentive observer, it becomes clear that the battle is not one that is merely against symbols of the products of racism, Islamophobia or on the other side, Islamic supremacism, but one for ethos: shaping one's own group and society. The battles, often physical in their consequences through acts of violence,[10] aim to define the 'human' within this context, to indeed determine the ethos, which the civilizers always see as degenerated and corrupted within their own environment. That is the reason for which Breivik murdered Norwegians and for which Malala Yousafzai (Yousafzai and Lamb 2013) was shot in the head by a faction of the Taliban for her advocacy to expand education among Afghan girls.

The clash of ethos is today very relevant since it is shaping Western countries, their Muslim minorities and also Muslim majority countries. A clear example of such battle, always marked by intolerance, is the case of the opposition of the Malay Muslim state to Christians using, as traditionally they have done, the term 'Allah' to refer to the biblical 'God'. Although a previous recent attempt to prevent Christians from using the word 'Allah' (Sankar 2013) failed, on 17 October 2013, a court finally imposed a ban on Christian publications using the name Allah for God.[11] Such an issue was rarely discussed in the past, and certainly courts never felt the need to intervene. Yet, with the start of the War on Terror, as we have seen elsewhere, Muslims in Malaysia started to suggest that Islam within the country may be threatened and that Christians were more active in converting Malay Muslims with money from the United States or in encouraging the Malay Muslims to be part of 'moderate Islam'. It does not help that some popular preachers, such as Mohd Hazizi Ab Rahman, foment such fear openly. A recent article[12] reported Ab Rahman speaking at the symposium 'Malay Leadership Crisis', which attracted a thousand-strong crowd. He was reported have said that whoever supports democracy, pluralism and human rights is a 'liberal Muslim' who the United States uses 'to make Muslims fight each other and bow down to them [the US and allies]'. The article also correctly reported that The Malaysia Islamic Development Department (JAKIM)[13] often reminds Muslims nationwide about the risks that Muslims face from the 'enemies of Islam' – enemies who attempt to brainwash good Muslims through dangerous ideas such as secularism, pluralism and positivism, among other philosophies – in its sermons for the Friday congregation.

The debate, through mass media and the internet, has become global, together with the arguments and rhetoric used, which include slogans and labels. 'Liberal Muslims', 'orthodox Muslims', 'jihadists', as well as 'Islamofascists', are all neologisms. These labels have increasingly made their appearance during the War on Terror as the result of both in-group and out-group clashes of ethos. Bourdieu (1987) has called 'symbolic power' the capacity to impose a vision of the social world. The tool used is stigma, and labels are perfect for stigmatizing others. According to Link and Phelan, three elements of Bourdieu's concept of symbolic power can help in understanding the power that stigma has:

> First, cultural distinctions of value and worth are the critically important mechanisms through which power is exercised. Stigma is in many respects a statement about value and worth made by a stigmatizer about those he or she might stigmatize and, thus, one form of symbolic power in Bourdieu's terms. Second, those who are disadvantaged by the exercise of power are often persuaded, sometimes without realizing it, to accept as valid the cultural evaluations that harm them. With respect to stigma, this is evident in the idea of 'internalized' or 'self' stigma. Finally, the exercise of symbolic power is often buried in taken-for-granted aspects of culture and thereby hidden, or 'misrecognized' as Bourdieu (1990) puts it, both by the people causing the harm and by those being harmed. (2013: 534)

Stigma affects always civilizers' rhetoric. Within the in-group, they aim to achieve 'self stigma', since in such a way homogenization may be achieved; stigmatization of out-groups is an essential part of the process of defining 'who is human'.

Conclusion

Many post-9/11 studies have questioned the position of Muslims about what many perceive as the 'core' values of the 'West'. Concepts such as secularism, democracy and freedom of speech were juxtaposed with fundamentalism, sharia and illiberalism. As we have seen, anthropologists have, in several influential studies, focused on Islam, seen in some cases as, mutatis mutandis, a blue print for social order and in others as a blue print for conduct. In other more recent studies, other more sophisticated analyses have attempted to observe Muslims in their everyday interactions with different social structures, such as secular societies or at least with a division between church and state of some sort, as we can find in some Muslim countries (see Malaysia, Indonesia, Turkey and so on) and Western countries. In these cases too, as seen in the formulation of *Islam mondain,* however, the focus remained not on the Muslims as actors but on Islam as a system. Most of the analyses that have identified Islam as one of the most 'fundamentalist' religions started from the assumption that the Enlightenment was a historical event of universal significance and that the War on Terror derived from the need to defend such values. In other words, the dynamics are clear: on one side the Muslims, unable to totally accept the deep intellectual importance of Enlightenment values, and on the other side the Western countries and intellectuals, inspired by and formed through such values.

Other studies have presented a different picture. For example, in a very recent article 'Secularism, Hermeneutics, and Empire: The Politics of Islamic Reformation', Saba Mahmood has embraced the view, held as we have seen by a great number of Muslims, that the West (in particular the US) is attempting to 'reshape' Islam; she concluded:

> I have suggested that contrary to normative understandings of secularism today, its force seems to reside not in neutralising the space of politics from religion but in producing a particular kind of religious subject who is compatible with the rationality and exercise of liberal political rule. In the current moment of empire, this aspect of secularism is most evident in the ambitious campaign the U.S. government has undertaken to reform and reshape Islam. (Mahmood 2006: 344)

This is not a very different position from, for instance, clerics such as Ab Rahman. Indeed, the fear that Islam is weak from the decadence of Muslims in their practice of religion is one of the most globalized arguments. Never have Muslims been, in history, so concerned about practices, dress code or sharia in its all different forms (normally matters of concern for specialized scholars and judges). Never before could terms such as 'orthodox' or 'liberal' Islam be observed in Muslim debates, and surely never before have Muslims so often accused others of being non-Muslim (or Shi'a Muslims, who are often considered non-Muslims by Sunni Muslims), a practice more and more common even in simple 'Facebook wars'. The same concerns that secularists had for Enlightenment values 'orthodox Muslims' have for Islam. It is clear that not only has the War on Terror uncovered the insecurity of postcolonial masters and the formerly colonized, but it has also opened the doors to an internal clash of values.

Indeed, in this chapter, I have concluded that the best way to understand the present situation is not to focus on the isolated elements, but to observe them as part of the same schismogenic process. When we start to analyse the debate in such a way, it becomes apparent that behind fragmented diatribes exists a clash of ethos. The clash is bi-dimensional, on one side there is the internal clash to impose a monolithic ethos upon the in-group, while on the other there is an external clash to impose the ethos upon the out-group, which is always seen as 'not human enough'. Only the acceptance of the correct, that is, civilized, ethos can save the opponent and in doing so, eschatologically save the 'human race'.

Notes

1 All names have been anonymized.

2 Traditional 'pulled tea' developed in India but popular among the Malay community, with sugar and condensed milk.

3 See the recent case of Alvin and Vivian, who posted photos of themselves wishing a happy Ramadan while eating Bak Kut Teh, which is made of pork, a food considered haram for Muslims, but allowed to be eaten by non-Muslims. For details, see: http://www.huffingtonpost.com/2013/07/18/alvin-and-vivian-jailed-malaysia-sex-bloggers_n_3616657.html (accessed 1 November 2013).

4 Ḥudūd (singular hadd) literally means limits. In Islamic law, it refers to specific offences mentioned in the Qur'an, which jurists see as offences against Allah instead of against humans or the state, and they require specific corporal punishments. Although the source of this legal tradition can be traced to the Qur'an, much of the hadd legislation is derived from historical juridical developments. For more information, see Mansour 1982.

5 This is the practice of consultation in an Islamic state. For more information, see Ayubi (1997).

6 Persatun Ulama Dan Guru-Guru Agama Islam Singapura (Singapore Islamic Scholars and Religious Teachers Associations).

7 See for instance the social political thought of Khan (2001).

8 It is interesting to notice how difficult it is to trace any academic study with titles or subtitles referring to minds and religions, such as, for instance, Christian minds, Jewish minds and so forth. See also Hassan (2008).

9 The Qur'an rejects such a possibility and describes Jesus only as a prophet.

10 See the EDL attacks on mosques and Muslims (Allen 2011) or Gianluca Casseri's assassination in December 2011 of two Senegalese vendors in Florence.

11 BBC article, 'Malaysia "Allah" court ruling: PM Najib speaks out': http://www.bbc.co.uk/news/world-asia-24621992 (accessed 22 October 2013).

12 The Malay Mail Online 'US colonising Malaysia through "liberal Muslims"': http://www.themalaymailonline.com/malaysia/article/us-colonising-malaysia-through-liberal-muslims-says-preacher#sthash.BE10ONix.dpuf.

13 JAKIM is a government body dedicated to the development and progress of Muslims in Malaysia: see http://www.islam.gov.my/en/about-jakim (accessed 1 October 2013).

4

Occidentalism, conspiracism and *jahiliyya*: Rhetoric of civilizational discourses

After the prayer we covered the few hundred metres that brought us back to the office where we continued our conversation. Amina spoke of women and morality in Malaysia: 'You see prof, the issue is that Muslims even here are exposed to Westernisation. The main issue is the body. I have studied at London School of Economics during my Masters and I could see there how sexualised young girls were. Not only were they covered in make up, but also the lack of modesty in their dress and behaviour was astonishing. That's why many of my Muslim brothers said that Western women are, in majority, equal to prostitutes.' She paused to watch for my reaction, then added, 'The hijab protects us from being like them. It reminds us of the duty of a Muslim woman and as a young woman. The temptations are many because of the Western way of life we live even in this country.'

At the food court, I had reached Fadhil, who was sipping his coffee while speaking of the situation in Afghanistan with some friends. In Singapore, there is not much discussion about the War on Terror and even less of the situation in Iraq and Afghanistan. It is a sensitive topic according to the government, and as in the case of many other sensitive topics, they were only really discussed at coffee shops if they were discussed at all. 'Do you know why the US is not winning in Afghanistan?' he asked with a rhetorical tone of voice. 'Because', he went on, replying to his own question after pausing for a sip of sweet milky coffee, 'many of the US soldiers are gay.' I asked him what sexuality had to do with the military operations over there. He looked surprised and said:

Gays are like women, right? They are effeminate and well, they are not good fighters. You see, what makes so many ang mohs (white people) gays is their culture. Western culture has some diseases, and homosexuality is one of the worst since it is spreading in the Muslim world to make it weak, feminine. Many Malays are into Western things, styles and then some of them then become gays. But look at what it does to a strong nation such as the US; look at them now, when they admitted gays in their military forces, they lost all wars.

Nassir is a lawyer who studied at the University of Melbourne. He is from a middle-class Lebanese background and in his thirties. During my research, we would often correspond over Facebook. On one particular day, the topic was about banks, mortgages and the financial crisis that has affected most of Europe. During some economic observations, he added,

The crisis is not just about bad economics, it is a very planned thing – it is an evil plan of the Jews and Israel. They as usual manipulated the financial order, and since they control the US, they created the crisis for their own interest and profit. Muslims should avoid Western banking, it is not safe. You know, even here in Australia, if you check carefully, you will see that most of the financial world and media are controlled by Jews and Israelis, who are really all the same right? They control everything.

In the aftermath of 9/11 and the subsequent 'War on Terror', discrimination against Muslims living in non-Muslim countries has increased exponentially, together with an atmosphere of suspicion and surveillance (Allen 2010). Academics studied such a phenomenon, and a vast literature within the humanistic and social scientific disciplines is available today.[1] Yet, scholars have conducted very little research and written even less about the effects that the War on Terror had on the conceptualization of the West among Muslims living in both Muslim and non-Muslim countries. Some research will point to the analysis of polls and surveys,[2] of which very few surveyed Muslim minorities living in Western countries. Qualitative research and, in particular, anthropological research on Muslims' attitudes towards non-Muslims and the West as an imagined category is lacking. Yet, any anthropologist who has conducted research among Muslim communities is aware of what we can call *occidentalism* (Buruma and Margalit 2004).

The War on Terror has not only increased and reshaped occidentalism as well as discrimination against Muslims, but, as we shall discuss in this chapter, also reinforced conspiracy theories. The study of 'conspiracism' in general is rather new and underdeveloped. Muslim conspiracism and conspiracism against Muslims is even less discussed. In the case of Muslim conspiracism, the few studies available focus on the Arab world and, as one may expect, the Middle East (for a discussion of the literature and its limitations, see Gray 2008). The studies that mentioned conspiracism within Western Muslim communities tend to examine it within the context of radicalism and fundamentalism. Yet, not all Muslims who put faith in conspiracy theories are radical or fundamentalist in their views of Islam or even politics. Quite the opposite, the majority are ordinary people who more often than not reject violence and condemn terrorist actions. This is also true for occidentalism: the majority expressing occidentalist stereotypes are not part of radical groups or indoctrinated in a specific way.

Hence, the relevance and, I would say, the urgency to understand the processes that facilitate both occidentalism and conspiracism. Indeed, although both are not directly related to radicalization or violent extremism, they may facilitate a *modus pensanti* which might, in the right context, become a *forma mentis* and, as such, initiate the radicalization process.

Occidentalism: Between stereotypes and imagination

As we have seen, scholarly research on Islamophobia has bloomed in the aftermath of 9/11 and the War on Terror. The reason is that discrimination and attacks against Muslims have increased to an exponential level. Much of the discrimination and intolerance towards Islam and Muslims is the result of fear, a fear that can find its archetype in the Ottoman army reaching the gates of Vienna (Marranci 2004; Malik 2009; Allen 2010; Shryock 2010). Yet, the study of what I can call 'the rhetoric of resentment' within Muslim communities, both in Western and non-Western countries, has remained unstudied at large. The reasons for such a lack of research are varied, although the perception of Muslims as victims within a certain sociopolitical environment may have facilitated the focus on only one side of the coin. The lack of studies on such a topic creates a significant gap in the effort to understand the dynamics of what we have called here the clash of civilizers within the context of the War on Terror.

In recent times, we can identify a few studies that have attempted to highlight the anti-Western rhetoric existing within Muslim communities. Although the majority of the academic literature in this field concentrates on anti-Semitism (see for more Jikeli and Allouche-Benayoun 2013; Ma'oz 2012), a few studies approach it from a more holistic perspective. One of such studies is the very much quoted *Occidentalism: The West in the Eyes of Its Enemies* (2004) by Ian Buruma and Avishai Margalit.

The study attempts to provide a reading of anti-Western rhetoric from a historical and political viewpoint. Buruma and Margalit have suggested that occidentalism, in other words, a dehumanizing picture of the West by its enemies, has its origin in the same thinking that characterized anti-Enlightenment movements in Europe, with their critique of scientism, excessive rationality, individualism, capitalism, city life and so on. Yet, occidentalism develops only when in the minds of enemies of the West and such critiques are adduced to one single factor, and that factor is expressed in geographical terms: The West. Indeed, the authors argue that occidentalism is historically an unavoidable product and consequence of close contact with Western ideas, culture and values. Occidentalism is, therefore, an inevitable aspect of modernity. Even the most critical forms of anti-Western ideas have, according to Buruma and Margalit, their origin in Western philosophy and political views. For this reason the authors refuse to see occidentalism as 'a peculiar Islamic problem', since, 'much has gone terribly wrong in the Muslim world, but Occidentalism cannot be reduced to a Middle Eastern sickness any more than it could to a specifically Japanese disease more than fifty years ago' (2004: 5).

Among the criticisms of Western values and ideas (i.e. Occidentalism), one is particularly commonly found among both 'born again Christians' and Islamists: the Western preference for humanistic values that limit, or in the worst case exclude, religion from public spaces. As Bilgrami has highlighted,

> The defining essence of the West lies in democracy and scientific rationality, but in the eyes of its enemies there is a conflation of these principles with the wider cultural phenomena. Perhaps the conflation occurs via some sort of *illicit derivation* of these cultural phenomena from those principles. Thus, occidentalism, in attacking the cultural phenomena, also attacks the West as defined by these principles. (2006: 284, italics in the original)

One of the most prominent principles, at the centre of Enlightenment, is the role of God in society, which in the West has been not only reduced but, one can say, has also been ostracized from the power of defining society. According to Buruma and Margalit, one of the main reasons 'the enemies of the West' accuse the West of feebleness, greed, decadence and sexual corruption is that 'the West, in the Occidentalist view, worships matter; its religion is materialism, and matter in the Manichaean view is evil. By worshiping the false god of matter, the West becomes the realm of evil, which spreads its poison by colonising the realm of the good' (2004: 7). As we shall see, one of the most used concepts to describe the West and the risk that it represents to the Muslim way life is the Arabic word *jahiliyya*.

Akeel Bilgram (2006) has acknowledged the relevance of Buruma and Margalit's study, in particular, for the attempt to find connections between previous historical phenomena of occidentalism and more recent examples, such as manifestations of it among Muslim communities. Yet, Bilgram has suggested that occidentalism is an intellectual work with a clear pedigree: the Cold War literature appealed to Christianity as something that defined the West, in contrast with the atheistic nature of communism – although this was done with a degree of sophistication when compared, for instance, with Huntington's 'clash of civilizations' thesis (as Bilgram notes: 'Its cold war voice comes with a veneer of balance') (Bilgram 2006: 386). Thus, for him, the occidentalism observed among Muslims, including those living in the West, is not irrational as some wish to demonstrate. Instead, it has its origin in the same West, as Buruma and Margalit suggest, yet not as an anti-Enlightenment force, but rather as a part of it.

> That tradition was clear-eyed about what was implied by the disenchantment of the world, to stay with the Weberian term. It is a tradition consisting not just of Gandhi and early seventeenth-century freethinkers, not just the Slavophile, Japanese, and German critics that are mentioned in their book, but a number of remarkable literary and philosophical voices in between that they don't discuss: Blake, Shelley, William Morris, Whitman, Thoreau, and countless anonymous voices of the nontraditional Left, the Left of the radical Enlightenment, from the freemasons of the early period down to the heterodox Left in our own time, voices such as those of Noam Chomsky and Edward Thompson and the vast army of heroic but anonymous organizers of popular grassroots movements – in a word, the West as conceived by the radical Enlightenment that has refused to be complacent about the orthodox Enlightenment's legacy of the thick rationality that early seventeenth-century dissenters had warned against. (Bilgram 2006: 402–3)

'Refusing to be complacent' explains, according to Bilgram, partly the violent manifestations that Muslim extremists have expressed against the West in 'fighting back against centuries of colonial subjugation; … the military and the corporate presence of the West (primarily the United States), which continues that subjugation in new and more subtle forms, out of their lands'. The idea of 'justice' is central to this discourse, as we shall see below.

Aydin (2006: 48) has suggested also that Western political ideas and philosophies, such as those of Max Horkheimer, Theodor Adorno, Jürgen Habermas, Michel Foucault and Herbert Marcuse had an impact on how the representation of the West has been formed among, for instance, Islamist groups. Funk seems to agree: 'Contemporary Islamic movements, for example, have assimilated the modern anti-imperialist discourse pioneered by socialists and early nationalist movements in colonised countries' (2004: 18). My research, in particular, in Australia, about Muslims' view of the West, has, more than in other countries, revealed a nearly Fanon (1963 and

1970) understanding of relations between Muslims and non-Muslims, with non-Muslims being identified by their 'white privilege'. It is not uncommon in Australia that even converts to Islam may be subjected to criticism and rejection because 'born Muslims' still perceive them as being part of the 'white privileged' Australian class and so part of the Occident. The discourse, even in this case, is a civilizational one. It is the action of the West that justifies, if not requires, resistance. As Funk correctly shows, 'This attitude comes complete with an array of images and associations that most Westerners would not regard as flattering, particularly in the areas of sexual morality, family life, crime, and public safety' (2004: 6).

The moral values, in particular, are often emphasized. For instance, many Muslims I have interviewed in different countries such as the UK, Singapore and Australia, have strongly linked non-heterosexuality to a 'Western disease' (see also Yip 2004). The civilizational discourse behind the expansion, particularly among young Muslims, of occidentalist rhetoric is demonstrated by further research, such as Appleton's study of attitudes of Muslims at British Universities, in which the author states 'interpretation of the dar al-Islam [the abode of Islam]/dar al-harb [the abode of the war, i.e. Christendom] dichotomy resonates with the respondents. ... Seddon (2001) describes such interpretations of dar al-Islam and dar al-harb as a form of Occidentalism, in that they involve an almost mythological demonization of all things Western' (2005: 308). My research has suggested that at the centre of such 'demonisation' and part of the civilizational discourse is the explicit or implicit concept of *jahiliyya*.

The concept of *Jahiliyya*

Being an anthropologist, neither the Qur'an nor the *hadiths* have introduced me to the term *jahiliyya*; rather it was Abu-Bakar, an elderly Libyan I had met in Paris. The man, who left Libya as a widower to join his son's family, used to say: 'Paris is *jahiliyya*, young people here live in *jahiliyya*, and even my son's home is full of *jahiliyya* stuff.' The Libyan grandfather could spot *jahiliyya* as easy as my grandfather could detect Penny Bun mushrooms in a thick Tuscan wood. Yet, Abu-Bakar shared other things with my often grumpy grandfather, such as his disapproving tone of voice as well as the rhythmical head shaking that emphasized condemnation of objectionable sights, and while in the process my grandfather used to exclaim 'indecent!', the Libyan man utters 'jahiliyya!'.

Although *jahiliyya* has been translated as a 'state of ignorance' (Netton 1992), the Arabic root *j-h-l* could also indicate '*barbarism*' (Izustsu 1966).

I had the impression that the Libyan grandfather used *jahiliyya* exactly to mean 'barbarism'; in fact, his '*jahiliyya*!' was equivalent to my grandfather's 'indecent!' The two men used these expressions to emphasize their feelings while comparing generational moral values. However, while my grandfather was comparing his generation's moral values against those of younger generations, the Libyan grandfather was comparing the moral values of his host society to a mythical, perfect, Islamic golden age modelled on the era of the Prophet Muhammad. Yet, it was not the figure of the Prophet, although much loved and honoured, which the Libyan saw as the essential difference between the perfect Islamic society and the secularized host society – rather, it was the sharia, the divine Islamic law.

The Qur'an mentions *jahiliyya* only four times (Sura 5:50, 3:154, 33:33, 48:26), all of them referring to pagan beliefs, paradigmatically symbolized by the lifestyle of the pre-Islamic rulers of Mecca, the Quraysh (cf. Sura 48: 26).[3] The Quraysh, as other pre-Islamic tribes, followed what was known as the 'Sunna', or the tradition established by the tribe's ancestors. The successful preaching of Muhammad not only established a new religion, Islam, but also disrupted the traditional tribal kinship system. In other words, Islam shifted the conception upon which law was formed in the Arabian Peninsula. The pre-Islamic law represented the efforts of the group to conserve traditions, while Islamic law represented the efforts of human beings to approach paradise on earth by doing what God wishes. In the Qur'an we can find sentences such as *afahukmal-jahiliyyati yabghun*, 'the law of pagan ignorance' (Sura 5:50, but see also Sura 3:154),[4] which suggests how the emphasis is in particular on the difference between the two forms of legislation. Although we can find the term *jahiliyya* mentioned only four times in the Qur'an, *jahiliyya* has a strong moral and ethical value, since it delimits two opposites: the corrupt pre-Islamic pagan world and the new Islamic, Muslim one (cf. Shepard 2001).

Nonetheless, during the history of the Islamic states, the term *jahiliyya* has acquired a political meaning that denotes a sharp distinction between Islamic and non-Islamic lands. This process probably started during the Abbasid dynasty, which ruled from 758 to 1258 and under which Islamic law (sharia) reached its full development (cf. Rina 1996). The newly born Islamic kingdom faced the hegemonic presence of Christian kingdoms in the Mediterranean as well as Eastern regions. Although mainly political, the struggle for the control of the region was presented as moral. In the case of the Islamic state, the concept of *jahiliyya* provided the moral emphasis to justify the earthly expansion of Islam. The Islamic state was supposed to wipe *jahiliyya* out of the human world. This, however, was only in theory, as history tells us that *jahiliyya* and Islam cohabited within the caliphate and within any subsequent Islamic governments.

Nonetheless, this did not prevent *jahiliyya* from becoming a powerful geopolitical-legal concept useful to the geopolitical distinction between *dar-al-Islam* and *dar-al-harb* of those times, though such dualistic division of the world exists neither in the Qur'an nor in the hadiths. Despite the strict Qur'anic emphasis (cf. Qu 2: 256) on war as self-defence and on religious tolerance and individual freedom, state rulers and leaders knew how to use interpretations of their religion to achieve political goals (Cook 2005). *Jahiliyya* became the centre of a sophisticated syllogism: since the Qur'an required Muslims to enjoin good and forbid evil (Qu 3: 104), and since non-Muslim lands lived under *jahiliyya* (i.e. did not recognize Islamic law), therefore Muslim states had the duty of calling non-Muslim states to Islam. If the invitation was declined, war against the *jahiliyyati* state was considered lawful.[5]

Notwithstanding Islamic history and the historical role that the idea of *jahiliyya* had in the dualistic division of the world into two antagonistic moral entities, we have to acknowledge that the concept of *jahiliyya* started to turn into something very different from what we may find in the Qur'an. Indeed, modern and contemporary Muslim scholars who consciously refer to *jahiliyya*, drawing on its theological and Islamic history heritage, have inevitably reshaped it through their experiences and historical contexts. This is evident in the writings of, for instance, Mawdudi[6] and, in particular, Sayyid Qutb.[7]

Mawdudi suggested the idea of 'the modern jahiliyya', arguing that his contemporary fellow Muslims, influenced by imperialist powers and secularist legislation, were betraying 'true Islam'; he urged them to struggle against 'paganism' as strongly as the Prophet and his companions struggled against the pagan Quraysh tribe. Sayyid Qutb followed Mawdudi in his argument, so that Shepard has concluded (2003: 535, italics in the original),

> Like the Qur'an, Qutb sees *jahiliyya* not as a past epoch but as a present reality. Like the Qur'an, Qutb's *jahiliyya* is closer to 'savagery' than to 'ignorance', although ignorance does seem to play somewhat more of a role for Qutb than for the Qur'an itself, given the place of science and the presence of atheism in the present *jahiliyya*.

Qutb developed what we may call a 'doctrine of jahiliyya' in advocating for the redemption of Muslims from dangerous Westernization. Qutb did not see *jahiliyya* as a technical word to describe pre-Islamic times. He charged the word with *anti-moral* (instead of immoral) and anti-ethical (instead of unethical) values, which we cannot find in the holy Muslim text. Qutb had applied his analogical thinking to the concept of *jahiliyya* and argued that only two opposite ethos exist: Islamic or *jahili*. Today, while only some Muslims might know and study Mawdudi's and Qutb's writing, the majority of Muslims use the concept of *jahiliyya*, or indirectly refer to it, while ignoring the political and theological debates surrounding it.

In an attempt to understand more about how contemporary Muslims use and understand the term *jahiliyya* and its derivatives, I have conducted some interviews with both migrants and Western-born Muslims living in Scotland. My respondents came from heterogeneous national, ethnic and Islamic backgrounds; yet their understanding of *jahiliyya* revealed some homogeneity in the idea that the West today embodies *jahiliyya*. This theorem (which often turned into an axiom) possessed its corollaries, even as my respondents elaborated their arguments differently.

Sadiq is a thirty-seven-year-old Pakistani man who migrated to England and shortly after moved to Edinburgh, where he has spent twelve years as an employee of several restaurants and kebab shops. Sadiq defined himself as a 'Friday-Muslim', meaning that he would attend the mosque for the obligatory collective prayer held each Friday in the local central mosque, but he was not generally 'mosque-going'. During our informal conversations and in-depth interviews, it became evident that Sadiq had little knowledge of Islamic history, jurisprudence (*fiqh*) and Qur'anic structure. Despite his lack of theological training, however, Sadiq held firm opinions about the meaning of *jahiliyya*. He confidently explained that he knew what *jahiliyya* was 'because I could see it everyday while serving kebab to my non-Muslim customers'. I came to know that *jahiliyya*, to Sadiq, was epitomized by young girls 'dressing immodestly, kissing with their boyfriends in public, swearing unchaste words, and showing no respect for God and their religion'. But *jahiliyya* was following Sadiq even at home when, in front of the television, he could feel his *iman* (inner religious faith) challenged by *jahili* advertisements, *jahili* films and *jahili* female presenters. Speaking to Sadiq, I began to have the impression that his interpretation of *jahiliyya* primarily meant 'immodesty'. I was wrong. Sadiq's idea of *jahiliyya* derived from his understanding of Islam. According to him, Islam 'is a matter of how-to-do rather than how-to-know'; or in other words, Islam is sharia, the Divine Law, the Supreme Guide. Sadiq believed that only under the sharia (self-imposed or state-enforced) could humans avoid *jahiliyya* and achieve justice. I could see how Sadiq's previous statement made logical sense: 'The West *is jahiliyya*, and this is because it lacks sharia.'

Adiba is a nineteen-year-old student at the University of Glasgow. She was born of Bangladeshi parents. Adiba wears a hijab and she describes herself as 'deeply religious but not fanatic because I have a modern approach to Islam'. She is involved in the Muslim student association of her university, and her use of hadith during our conversations implied that she had a better Islamic education than Sadiq. Adiba used the word *jahiliyya* quite often when addressing new 'sisters' joining the 'Muslim women's circle', where she would sometimes find herself advising them: 'Muslim girls have to avoid the *jahili* behaviour that they see in their non-Muslim friends since the Qur'an says, "He or she who does not judge by what God has revealed is an unbeliever" [cf. Qu 5:44].' During an interview, Adiba explained that in the hadiths, *jahiliyya* refers to any pagan behaviour; she then observed,

> In the West the majority of people are only interested in money and sex. In this society, affected by fanatic secularism, women prefer their jobs to their families. If you observe this society, we see that there are many divorces; this is because many women, when they are young, date lots of men and have fun. Then they marry and they find it boring because they are used to booze and have sex with people they don't know. Women in this society no longer have any moral guide. They look for pleasure and they suffer a lot. This country [Scotland] should be Christian and having Christian laws, but in reality we are living in a *jahili* [pagan] society.

However, like Sadiq, Adiba believed that *jahiliyya* had an impact not only on moral values but also on political decisions. The example she cited to support this point was the recent military conflict in Iraq:

> The Americans do not have real moral values. What they want is oil, power, and to control the global economy. They do not have interest in what is God's Will; they use religion but do not serve God. So, in Iraq they kill and torture, without mercy, innocent Muslims. Like the pagans, people in the West do not fear the Day of Judgment, so they enjoy *haram* [forbidden] things.

Adiba, though less explicitly than Sadiq, also seemed to suggest a relationship between *jahiliyya* and a lack of justice. This relationship finally became clear to me while discussing the topic with Afeef.

Afeef was a twenty-six-year-old man of Pakistani origin living in Glasgow, when I met him. Wishing to study Islamic jurisprudence, in order to become a trained imam, he had applied to the Muslim College of London. His lifestyle and his appearance confirmed his strong faith: long beard, neatly trimmed moustache, *thobe* (traditional tunic), *Pakol* (traditional Afghan hat) and a (very Western) padded jacket to protect himself from the biting Scottish winter cold. Afeef believed that the lifestyle he was following (from dress to diet) was the Prophet's perfect path (Sunna) and he was dismissive of any other Islamic style (which he defined as *bida*, i.e. innovation or heresy). In other words, Afeef's Islam was *the Islam*. His preamble to our first conversation made it clear:

> There is one Islam only: the Islam of the Prophet. Some Muslims think that Islam should be interpreted; they are wrong, completely wrong. They wish and preach *bida*. If you do not like what Islam says, it means that you

are worse than a non-Muslim, you are one of the *mushrikin* [hypocrites]. If you want to know what will happen to them, just read the Qur'an. I am too scared to even tell you. You see, Islam means submission to Allah and not submission to personal ego and pleasure.

Afeef's Islam meant total submission, beyond human reason, to Allah's will. Afeef expressed again this concept saying, 'Muslims have to reach, within themselves, *al-fitra*,' and explained that *al-fitra*, though it may be translated as 'human nature', has a specific theological significance. He told me that all humans beings are born in the state of *fitra*, and quoted a hadith from al-Bukhari, 'No child is born except on *al-fitra*.' Thus, Afeef explained, 'The state of *al-fitra* is nothing else than the perfect state of Islam. Children contain in themselves the Divine Law; all of us are born Muslims and then corrupted.' Afeef observed that the duty of each Muslim is to rediscover and go back to that perfect Islamic spiritual essence. This argument became the key point to understanding Afeef's idea of *jahiliyya*.

According to Afeef, today we live in an oxymoronic state between *al-fitra* and *jahiliyya*; we have Islam but we can choose *jahiliyya*, as the Meccan pagans did. He observed that those pagans hoped to subjugate their false gods through spells and magic rituals, and added, 'They employed poetry, music and promiscuous sex. For this reason these things are *haram* [forbidden] in Islam.' The main struggle in this spiritual battle between *jahiliyya* and Islam may be expressed through one word: justice. Indeed, Afeef stated: 'Only total submission to *al-'hakam* [The Judge] and *al-'adl* [The Just] could give us peace and joy.' Since he had an interest in becoming a professional imam, Afeef expressed his ideas with some theological sophistication. Although my other respondents have presented a less clear theological argument, we can still observe that *jahiliyya* has been related to the idea of injustice or, as we shall see later, a-justice.

Conspiracy theories and civilizational fears and strategies

'There is evidence', – these words appeared in my small Facebook Chat window – 'it is not fiction, the vaccine is in reality a weapon and it has been used before against poor Muslims in Africa. Now they are doing the same in Pakistan.' I struggled to believe that a university-educated, second-generation Pakistani living in the UK could accept such a conspiracy theory. 'They fear the Muslim demographic wave. It is inevitable, Muslims will outnumber Christians and they want to stop this.' How? Tauseef has no doubts: 'They have polluted the polio vaccine with a chemical that provokes infertility.' The conspiracy theory surrounding the polio vaccination developed among the Muslim population of Kenya in 2003, after five years of successful vaccination programmes. The result was devastating in that the programme started to fail. Worse still, the conspiracy theory spread, affecting Muslim communities in India. The day he contacted me on Facebook, Tauseef was discussing the latest development: the systematic killing of whoever was connected to polio programmes in Pakistan. As I write, at least seven people have been killed and eleven injured in a bomb attack on a police van transporting vaccination teams.[8] Two days ago, gunmen opened fire in the Qayumabad area, killing one man and two women administering polio drops.[9] Tauseef had no problem in justifying the attacks, although he suggested that the campaign should avoid human victims and focus on sabotage only, 'What can Muslims do? Crusaders have sophisticated systems to attacks us. We do not have the same advantages. We should defend ourselves and Islam.'

Discussing with a group of Muslims in Sydney, in their late thirties, about the fact that HIV is spreading among young people and also affecting Muslims, mainly because of a lack of condom use and the exchange of syringes for steroid injections at gyms among young men, I was openly told of how HIV was actually spread by the US government through Christian missionaries.[10] Again, the conspiracy theory suggests that the West, and by extension Christianity, attempts to kill or destroy Muslims because, as one Lebanese man in the group explained, 'It is only through weakening Muslims, killing them, that the Christian West can prevent Islam from being the only religion. But Allah knows the best. There is nothing they can do.'

The alleged attempts by the West to weaken Islam can be found everywhere, even in the current Egyptian political turmoil that started with the Arab Spring. Unsurprisingly, like the other conspiracy theories, what is developed in the Middle East also reaches Muslim communities in the West. Rumours and allegations suggesting that the Muslim Brotherhood was tainted by a secret allegiance to the Jews and Israel spread to such an extent that in the streets of Cairo, during the anti-Morsi protests, one could hear the chant 'Khaibar, Khaibar, oh Jews, the Brothers are the Jews', which is a variation of an anti-Semitic chant, 'Khaibar, Khaibar, oh Jews! The army of Muhammad will return!',[11] often chanted by Hamas members in Palestine during the Intifada.

Of course, among the conspiracy theories I have encountered within Muslim communities, some have been very widespread also among the general population. This is the case of the allegations that 9/11 was an 'internal job' and that some 4,000 Jews did not attend work on the morning of the attack (in reality, between 400 and 500 people of Jewish descent were killed in the attacks). There were also conspiracy theories about Osama bin Laden and Saddam Hussein. The only difference is that among Muslims from the Middle

East, South and Southeast Asia, as well as, of course, among Muslims living in Western countries, the numbers of those who report, believe and defend such theories are higher than the general population (Gray 2008). For example, overall, in the United States 11 per cent of voters (this includes Muslim voters) believe that the US government allowed 9/11 to happen,[12] yet a Pew Global research suggested that 'there is no Muslim public in which even 30% accept that Arabs conducted the attacks' (Pew Research Centre 2011: 6).

Some other conspiracy theories that scholars may encounter in Muslim online forums, or see repeated several times on Facebook are, among many others, that Zionists are spreading homosexuality (apparently to control the world), that the Coca-Cola logo, when reversed, states in Arabic 'No Muhammad, No Mecca', and that Pepsi and Coca Cola contain pork-derived substances. As I discovered one day while dining with a Muslim friend, not even Coca-Cola's competitor was safe from conspiracism: the name Pepsi is not an innocent label but rather a strong reminder for the supporters of Israel: 'Pay Each Penny Save Israel.' Of course, this meant that Pepsi's profit would be redirected, as my friend pointed out while suggesting that we just have a lemonade, to finance new colonies in Palestine.

We can say that, for each conspiracy theory Muslims may hold about the West, Christianity and Western capitalism, there is one in which Islam is the target. The list is long and rather well documented (contrary to the study of Muslim conspiracism). Anti-Islam conspiracies are a kind of mirror of the ones we have discussed above. If a large number of Muslims in the world fear that the 'Christian West' is attempting to get rid of Islam once and for all, an equally large number of non-Muslims worldwide, particularly in the United States, believe the opposite. The sharia law and 'sneak Islamization' conspiracy theories are the most common, not just on blogs, Facebook and in general talks, but also even in political debate. For instance, Siv Jensen, the leader of the populist right-wing Progress Party in Norway used 'sneak-Islamization' in 2009 (Sandberg 2013). This conspiracy theory is a development of a well-established concept, even in some corners of academia, called Eurabia. The argument of Gisèle Littman, otherwise known as Bat Ye'or (an Hebrew pseudonym meaning 'daughter of the Nile'), is straightforward: Islam means submission, all contemporary Muslims dream of forcing non-Muslims into submission and transforming them into *dhimmi* – who are second-class oppressed citizens in her conceptualization of the term (Ye'or 2002). Muslims conduct two jihads, one violent and criminal and the other manipulative, in trying to Islamicize the European political Left. This is the gist of Bat Ye'or's main argument. Recently, she has concluded,

Europe's hidden war against Israel is wrapped in the Palestinian flag, and is part of a global movement that is transforming Europe into a new continent of dhimmitude within a world strategy of jihad and da'wa, the latter being the pacific method of Islamization. The implementation program of this policy of dhimmitude for the Euro-Arabian continent [sic] is set forth in the Rapport du Comite de Sages submitted to the European Commission President Romano Prodi in October 2003. This program, entitled 'Dialogue between Peoples and Cultures in the Euro-Mediterranean region' was accepted by the European Union in December 2003. Unfortunately, the policy of 'Dialogue' with Arab League nations, wilfully pursued by Europe for the past three decades, has promoted European dhimmitude and rabid Judeophobia. (Bat Ye'or 2004)

These same ideas have been expressed by commentators and anti-Jihad celebrities such as Robert Spencer[13] and, as we have observed in the previous chapter of this book, inspired Anders Behring Breivik (Fekete 2012) in his own terrorist actions. Fekete's article (2012, in particular, 39–44) provides a list of these persistent conspiracies.

Rep. Peter T. King's call for a US Congress Hearing (which was held on 10 March 2011) to discuss the place of Muslims in American society may provide an idea of how far the idea of 'Islamization' and 'shariafication' have gone, together with the criminalization of an entire community, despite the usual disclaimer that 'we are speaking only of a few extremists' (Fahrenthold and Boorstein 2012). It is then not surprising that books such as *Muslim Mafia: inside the secret underworld that's conspiring to Islamize America* (Gaubatz and Sperry 2009) are widely read and commented upon.[14]

Auper has correctly noticed that 'traditionally, the social sciences have tended to either neglect or morally condemn conspiracy culture' (2012: 23). Anthropological research on conspiracy theories is rare and lacking in many respects (West and Sanders 2003). Anthropological research concerning conspiracy theories existing among Muslim communities in the West or affecting Muslim communities in the West is practically non-existent.[15] Several other disciplines within the humanities and social sciences have researched the phenomenon (Franks, Bangerter and Bauer 2013), such as cultural studies (e.g. Parish and Parker 2001), psychoanalytic studies (e.g. Zonis and Joseph 1994), political science (the famous study by Hofstadter 1965), history (Roberts 1972), philosophy (Keeley 1999) and psychology (Swami et al. 2011). Franks, Bangerter and Bauer have also complained that 'whilst insightful, such research has investigated CTs from within a discipline, focusing either on symbolic aspects (e.g. rhetoric, discourse, narratives; Billig 1987) or on psychological phenomena (cognitive biases and errors, individual differences, psychopathology), but there have been few attempts at integration – leaving a more general theory of CTs [conspiracy Theories] lacking' (2013: 1).

Byford (2011) and Keeley (1999) have noticed that scholars tend to agree on what the label 'conspiracy theory' indicates; yet this confidence in the self-explanatory meaning of the label has meant that some avoid any real definition (see, for instance, Butler, Koopman and Zimbardo 1995). Conspiracy theories are unverified claims which are more implausible than the official explanation, aim to surprise, and assume that everything that happened is planned for an evil or damaging intent despite the fact that they are based on weak evidence, so that any questioning or doubt is rejected (Brotherton 2013).

Notwithstanding the agreement on what conspiracy theories are, scholars have different views on what produces them and why they exist. According to Stempel, Hargrove and Stempel (2007), social scientific studies of conspiracy theories can be classified in mainly two ways. The more psychological first approach suggests that 'there is a conspiratorial personality or paranoid style of thought, and views conspiracy theories as closely related to scapegoating and "us versus them" worldviews' (2007: 357). This is clearly derived from the 1950s' Hofstadter's studies (1960), which also advanced the hypothesis that conspiratorial thinking prevails among marginalized people within a society (such as women, minorities and youth) as well as isolated or powerless groups. Some scholars still support the paranoid origin of conspiracy theories (Darwin, Neave and Holmes 2011; Swami et al. 2011) and as we shall see, students of the phenomenon in the Middle East and Arab world have employed such analytical explanations (Zonis and Joseph 1994; Pipes 1996, 1997). Stempel et al. have named the second approach 'cultural sociology' because of its 'emphasis on the social structuring of beliefs and its social relativist bracketing of the truth claims of conspiracy theories' (2007: 355). In this case, paranoia has not so much to do with the formation and spread of conspiracy theories, which are not seen as illogical, but rather to do with the rational attempt to react to a modern society marked by high risks in different spheres of life.

Aupers (2012: 31) strongly supports the view that conspiracy theories are not irrational or a product of a deviant state of mind, but are instead a result of modernization and what Max Weber describes as 'the bureaucratisation of life':

> Setting aside essentialist questions about whether or not conspiracy theories are really rational – questions that are in the end informed by moral-political perspectives – we may assess that this growth and normalization of conspiracy theories are not a symptom of resignation, as critical modernists would have it, but of cultural transformation in the West – of 'cultural rationalization' (Weber 1978). It is a mainstay that many modern institutions and social structures have lost much of their plausibility for ordinary people – particularly since the 1960 and 1970s (e.g. Berger et al. 1973; Campbell 2007). Motivated by this, conspiracy theorists actively

produce and reconstruct (ultimate) cultural meaning by blending a high degree of rationalism with a strong feel for the metaphysical.

Others have suggested that conspiracy theories are the result of political cynicism (Swami, Chamorro-Premuzic and Furnham 2010; Swami et al. 2011) and a form of defence against out-groups (Kofta and Sedek 2005), particularly when, as Newheiser, Farias and Tausch (2011: 1011) have proposed, it allows 'people to alleviate or cope with threats to their sense of meaning and control'.

While the studies focusing on Muslims and conspiracism are few, several of them are extremely problematic. Zonis and Joseph (1994) may be considered as one such example, and one that has influenced others, such as Pipes (1996, 1997). The gist of their argument is that

> conspiracy thinking is a form of paranoid-like thinking or reasoning that occurs especially in response to stressors that evoke either experiences of traumatic passivity, a repetition of disintegration anxiety first experienced in childhood …, or frustration or incompetence in negotiating social situations under stress. … Conspiracy thinking as compared with paranoia entails additional factors. In a sense, the notion of the individual must be expanded to include peoples and their cultures. (1994: 453)

The two authors continue to focus on what they think are the child-rearing practices of Arabs and Muslims (all of them!) and identify as 'the role of secrecy in society; and attitudes toward sexuality, in particular the degree to which sexuality (especially homosexuality) is shrouded in secrecy and the degree to which certain sexual experiences are associated with passivity' (1994: 453). The argument advanced is clearly grounded in stereotypes and what has been identified as orientalist discourse. They conclude that conspiracy theories in the Muslim world can be explained with what Devereux (1980) called an 'ethnicpsychosis', derived in this case from the shock of the contact with Western modernization, which has challenged their traditional way of life. Muslims, seemingly because of their child-rearing practices, are not ready to cope with such changes and this brings about the creation of conspiracy theories as an attempt to gain control of the changing environment.

Zonis and Joseph's argument, though interesting, is fully a part of the civilizational discourse that we are debating in this book. They dehumanize Arabs, Iranians and Muslims in general by transforming them into monolithic cultural objects who are affected by a psychosis created by their 'uncivilized', 'anti-modern', 'irrational' and 'anti-enlightenment' culture and religion. Unsurprisingly, Pipes has reproduced most of Zonis and Joseph's argument and adopted the pathological approach (Stempel, Hargrove and Stempel 2007). Pipes' work suffers from an exaggerated reductionism, a serious 'othering' and despite providing a good list of conspiracies, particularly those affecting Jews and Masons, the paranoia paradigm is unconvincing.

A recent cognitive theory of conspiracism may prove more useful in understanding the similar yet opposed occidentalist and anti-Islam conspiracy theories that we have observed above. Franks, Bangerter and Bauer (2013) have advanced the hypothesis that contemporary theories incorporate in their narrative some counter-intuitive representations of external agents who know everything and control everything concerning the event. They also have noticed that 'ascribing supernormal agency to the conspirators connects the conspiracy to historical inter-group relations and conflicts, so that the social groups involved are also represented in hard-to-falsify essentialist terms, which naturalize the differences and explanation' (2013: 9). According to the authors, this contributes to the management of psychological anxiety by 'translating diffuse anxiety about a threat into specific, historically recurrent fears and inter-group dynamics. … Widespread conspiracy theories (CTs) should typically involve easily identified outgroups, either in stigmatized minorities or powerful elites whose agency is implicated and exaggerated' (ibid.).

What we can call civilizational conspiracism fits the cognitive hypothesis of Franks et al. The counterposed conspiracies are the result of the fear that an external threat can change, alter and, in particular, annihilate one's 'way of life', or what we have called ethos, which civilizers consider the only way to be 'human'. Indeed, anti-Islam conspiracy theories represent Islam (and so Muslims) as a kind of supernormal agency able to jeopardize the freedom and 'values' of the West. Equally, 'Muslim civilisers' fear that their religion, Islam, is threatened by this supernormal agency called the West and Western values (or better anti-values), which through medicine, technology, sex, homosexuality and so on seeks to annihilate the only way to be human: to be Muslim.

In the aftermath of 9/11 and the consequent War on Terror, conspiracism became part of the arsenal of those I have referred to in this book as civilizers. Although conspiracy theories have always existed, something has changed in how they are used. We have seen how the idea that the West aims to substitute 'real Islam' with a more pleasing counterfeit is incredibly popular among many Muslims and, in some cases, even scholars. The terrain is fertile for the civilizers among the respective communities to not only have a strong voice, but also to use conspiracy theories to manage psychological anxiety by 'translating diffuse anxiety about a threat into specific, historically recurrent fears'. It is this particular effect of conspiracy theories that is the most appreciable, effective and definitely dangerous since, as I have explained in Chapter 2, although we do not have a clash of civilizations per se, we have individuals and groups that try their very best to have one. Indeed, to them, it is only through a 'final' clash that the threat to the 'real civilization' can be deflected and humanity saved from the barbarians.

Conclusion

The War on Terror and its consequences have been analysed from many perspectives: their geopolitical impact, their military aspects, the reduction in civil liberties and the discrimination of Muslims (or the so-called Islamophobia). Yet, very little has been written about how the War on Terror has tarnished the image of the West among Muslims or how it has facilitated the formation of parallel conspiracy theories. I have suggested in this book that what we are witnessing today is not a clash of civilizations, but rather a clash of civilizers. In this chapter, we have analysed some of the rhetoric and arguments that civilizers use in the attempt to impose their idea of what it means to be human. It is important to understand that for civilizers, the fear, the sense of threat and insecurity are real and emotionally pervasive. The imagined West within occidentalist rhetoric and narrations is not just the 'other', or merely the 'opposite' of Islamic culture, as again imagined by the Muslim civilizer. Rather, the West in occidentalist representations is the epitome of human decadence, the anti-human.

Implicitly or explicitly, *jahiliyya* is a relevant concept that helps link the occidentalist rhetoric, which would otherwise not be acceptable to a majority of Muslims, to the Qur'an. Through this link, the rhetoric becomes more palatable to a wider Muslim audience: the idea that the West is *jahiliyya* and its values are *jahiliyya* is easily arguable and then becomes relatively acceptable to them. Yet, this also facilitates the division of the world into two spheres: one where Islam, through sharia, is applied and present, and the other which is secular and Christian at the same time and, in particular, a place where the law is guided by the will of men instead of the divine, and so originating in *jahiliyya*. It is not difficult to see how such an argument may add stress to Muslims living in Western countries.

Yet, it is not just Muslims living in the West who are affected. Muslim conspiracy theories transform the West, Christianity and secularism into super-agents of sorts, which are perfectly suited to creating a threat that is cognitively acceptable and functional in the creation of a powerful out-group. More and more conspiracies are spread globally and some with disastrous consequences, as the polio conspiracies demonstrate. Yet, this helps to reinforce the perception of being under attack, where the attack is not aimed at conquering a land or resources but instead the very souls of Muslims. Unsurprisingly, as a kind of mirror, anti-Islam conspiracies work in an identical way, only it is not the soul or religion that these civilizers fear to lose but rather their ideas of what it means to be human: freedom, secularism and individualism.

Notes

1 Although a rather inaccurate way of evaluating the quantity of literature, a Google Books search by title reveals 5,700 books with Islamophobia mentioned in the title; similarly, a Google Scholar search reveals 15,000 journal articles with Islamophobia mentioned in the title.

2 LaFree and Morris (2012), McCauley and Stellar (2010), Tessler and Robbins (2007), Panagopoulos (2006) and Tessler (2003).

3 The Quraysh were also the bitter enemies of the Prophet.

4 All Qur'anic quotations are from Asad (2004).

5 This did not mean that they had to attack or conquer all the non-Muslim regions, but rather that one day those lands would be brought under Islam see Marranci (2006).

6 Mawdudi (1903–79) has been an influential Islamic reformist. He founded the Islamic organization Jama'at al-Islami.

7 Sayyid Qutub (1906–66) has been one of the most prominent figures of the Muslim Brotherhood and revivalist movement.

8 Los Angeles Times, 23 January 2014, http://www.latimes.com/world/worldnow/la-fg-wn-pakistan-polio-attacks-20140122,0,5287845.story (accessed 23 January 2014).

9 BBC, 21 January 2014, http://www.bbc.co.uk/news/world-asia-25823154] (accessed 23 January 2014).

10 The conspiracy that HIV was spread by US missionaries was mentioned by the cleric Khalid Yasin during a visit to Australia in 2005 which attracted media interest.

11 Khaibar was the name of the last Jewish village which Muhammad defeated in 628, officially ending an organized Jewish presence in Arabia.

12 See Public Policy Report 2 April 2013, http://www.publicpolicypolling.com/pdf/2011/PPP_Release_National_ConspiracyTheories_040213.pdf (accessed 21 January 2014).

13 Spencer is also an author of books spreading anti-Islamic conspiracies in the United States, such as Spencer (2008).

14 For a criticism of the book, see Kumar (2010).

15 Even a simple search in the journal *Annual Reviews of Anthropology* produces zero results.

5

'Your women are oppressed, but ours are awesome': Civilizers and gender[1]

Women as a civilizational litmus test

At a cafe in Russell Square in London, which had become one of my 'offices' for interviews, I met with four young Londoners of Pakistani heritage, who had agreed to discuss with me their ideas concerning the West, democracy and Islam. Although they were young men (Ahmad, aged nineteen, Dawood, twenty-three, Faisal, twenty and Hafeez, twenty-one), they had clear ideas of what they liked and disliked of that geopolitical-social West in which they were born to first-generation Pakistani parents. We were not seated long before a female student from The University of London School of Oriental and African Studies (SOAS) passed close to the table dressed in summer clothes, exposing her midriff and legs. The SOAS student attracted the attention of my respondents. Themselves cleanly shaven and sporting jeans and t-shirts that revealed enough to suggest they all had gym memberships, they seemed particularly focused on the 'Westernness' of the female student's dress style.

Dawood, the oldest of the group, was the first to notice the student and gestured to attract my attention towards her and said, 'Here you are Doc, that's an example of what does not work in the West.' It was not difficult for me and the others to identify the subject of the remark. Ahmad agreed, 'Yeah, if she were Muslim her father would not let her go out like that – nor would I if I were her brother!' Hafeez added, 'You know, they do not have modesty, you can see everything and this provokes men.' The comparison with Muslim women seemed inevitable. The four young men identified in the dress style and behaviour of Western non-Muslim women the antithesis of the idea of the 'right' woman. The dehumanization and reduction became evident when Dawood spoke about the jokes among his Muslim friends about white non-Muslim women, and how they highlighted the lack of decency, the fact that they were easy and without morals. Yet, the others pointed out that this was not the fault of the woman per se but that of 'Western culture'. Indeed, Faisal reminded us, 'Western culture is not like Islam. It is the opposite. Even some of our sisters [i.e. Muslim women] end up being corrupted.'

Discussions of Muslim women often venture into terrains of controversy and Australia is no unique exception. Discussions about Australian Muslim women attract media, academic and political attention as well as the attention of groups actively opposing the 'spread of Islam' in the country. For instance, one of the most reproduced photos in newspaper articles discussing veiling in Australia is Sergio Redegalli's anti-burqa mural,[2] which he denied was anti-Islam or anti-Muslim in its message that the burqa is anti-Australian. According to reporters, Mr Redegalli drives a car bearing a sticker saying, 'Australians have nothing to hide, say no to burqas.' Facebook groups have also been opened with the name 'Ban the Burka in Australia',[3] containing posts suggesting again the difference between the 'Australian' and 'Islamic' ways of life, with particular reference being made to the perceived oppression of Muslim women compared to Australian women. Among the most aggressive websites, which often focus on Muslim women and their veiling, is the supposedly satirical 'Winds of Jihad' by Sheik Yer'mami as well as the homepage of the Australian Defence League.[4] Similar organizations and campaigns can be found in other Western countries.

The members of these organizations are heterogenous, part of different political movements, which are normally but not always from the extreme Right, and they are varied in their ideas and approaches to their identified enemy: the spread of Islam. I have conducted some interviews, mainly through internet chat conversations, since many do not want to reveal their identity, with some of these members. Although some are clearly racist, hateful and part of extreme right-wing parties, to label all of them 'Nazis' would be a mistake. Even the rather generic term Islamophobia may not fully represent the reasons that a large number of these individuals join such extreme anti-Muslim groups. Indeed, many are not against Islam per se or even against Muslims. Instead, a great number resent the 'infiltration' of what they have perceived to be a threatening 'alien culture incompatible with our civilisation'. For example, Jake, a forty-year-old teacher, is quick to reply,

No, I do not have problems with Muslims. I have Muslim students in my school and I see them as all the other students. I have problems, however, with the values Muslims advocate and in some cases want to impose on non-Muslims and Muslim women as well. If Muslims saw their religion as a personal matter, the situation would be different. Yet, you know better than me, this is not the case. Islam is an ideology.

Gender, as we shall see in this chapter, is central to the clashing rhetoric of civilizers, particularly during the War on Terror. Yet, it is not just 'women' who attract the attention of those wishing to demonstrate that their way of life is the correct way of being human. Indeed, masculinity and non-heterosexuality are also part of the arsenal of the civilizational rhetoric. Nonetheless, in the case of women, we can trace a precise historical genealogy of the rhetoric of civilization.

Enlightenment, colonialism, empires and the narrative of civilizing women

Mazlish (2004: 157) has noticed that 'in almost all discussions of civilisation since its conceptualisation by Mirabeau, the status of women has been mooted as the measure of the level of civilisation'. Similarly, Towns has also observed, 'The political empowerment of women has thus become understood as closely tied to so-called "Western civilisation". Indeed, few indicators seem more effective in signalling the civilisational standing of a state than the situation of women' (2009: 682). Yet, which role women had to have in the civilizational mission was debated:

> Some, such as Kant, have assigned to the female sex the task of civilizing men. James Mill, though scornful of women in actuality and denying them the right to vote – claiming that their interests were already represented by their husbands – declared that how they were treated represented the dividing line between barbarism and civilization. His son, John Stuart Mill, although horrified by some of his father's opinions, nevertheless agreed that the status of women was the measure of civilization, and called for a domestic revolution. Both Freud and Nietzsche, although deeply suspicious of women, nevertheless recognized their critical role in civilization. (Mazlish 2004: 157)

Socialist utopian Fourier is mentioned as being the first to make a direct connection in 1808 between the position of women within a society and the level of civilization of that society: 'Social progress and changes of historical period take place in proportion to the advance of women toward liberty, and social decline occurs as a result of the diminution of the liberty of women' (cited in Beecher 1990: 1).

Yet, the reality is rather more complex than the imagined idea that the West was a champion of women's rights, thanks to the Enlightenment and secularism. Towns (2007, 2009) has highlighted that if we compared Europe in the nineteenth century with the medieval period or with the Renaissance, we can observe an exclusion of women from the political sphere only in the nineteenth century. It would be only after long battles for political rights much later that European women could be part of politics again. As Bock (2002) and others (Laqueur 1990; Riley 1988) have argued, the Greek philosophical idea that sex and gender were the variation of a single human prototype continued to have an impact in the conceptualization of women as 'lesser men', rather than distinctive beings, in the sixteenth and seventeenth centuries (Towns 2009: 688). Class and status proved more relevant than the category of gender, so that women were much more involved in politics. Yet, in the eighteenth century, the two-sex model which identified men and women as ontologically different prevailed, and this, Towns argues, 'made it possible to speak about women as a collective. This also made it possible to ban "woman" *as such* from the state polity, based on her distinctive characteristics' (2009: 684). Hence, women became inferior beings instead of simply different and, perhaps on average, weaker in physical strength. To put it another way, the weakness presumed in women in the eighteenth century was not on account of a lack of strength – as it had been earlier – but instead on account of intelligence.

Hall and Jackson have noticed that 'the exclusion of women from the political sphere was held forth as indicative of a more civilised society – European scholars and politicians contended and showed that only "savage" societies ceded political power to women' (2007: 168).[5] Towns is correct in suggesting that in precolonial Africa and Asia we can find, as anthropologists reported, women involved, at different levels, in politics and in some cases possessing power through matrilineal kinship. Yet, colonial authorities in their 'civilisational' efforts disrupted or eradicated such realities and only male leaders were often acknowledged or imposed (Parpart 1988; Sacks 1982). To be civilized meant to have the right social order: to have men in charge of politics, and women in charge of the domestic space, which was represented as the most appropriate for women to advance civilization: 'No universal agent of civilization exists but our mothers' (Aimé-Martin 1843: 228; cited in Towns 2007: 176).

Nonetheless, the same eighteenth- and nineteenth-century intellectuals justified colonization through, among other things, a rescue operation to save 'brown' and 'black' women since 'the condition of woman has always been the most degraded the nearer we approach to a state of nature, or, rather, the less we are raised above the level and mere animal characteristics of the brute creation' (Fullom 1855: 149; cited in Towns 2009: 702). Towns has identified the contradiction which existed in these views since 'women were thus simultaneously most in need of civilization, in order to be raised out of degradation and protected from sheer force, and yet they posed a challenge to civilization's creation and maintenance' (Towns 2009: 996). Not surprisingly, some scholars (Inglehart and Norris 2003), including, as Towns reminds readers, feminists (Burton 1990; Ramusack 1990; Strobel 1991), have suggested appearances of Western superiority in the treatment of women, in some cases, even during colonization. Clearly, today's parameters to evaluate civilization and the consequent civilizational rhetoric not only focus on the protection of women from brutal force, but also extend to full emancipation, political rights, sexual rights and so forth. In other words, the West saved women from barbarian cultures and societies.

In the following sections, we shall observe how this discourse is not just limited to Western civilizers. Evaluating the condition of women as a measure of the moral and civil advancement of a society can be found in discussions among the Ottoman Empire's Muslim intellectuals, and of course, the rhetoric here is inverted. On the one hand, Muslim women are seen as the prototype of the civilized woman who has benefited from the advancement and justice of Islam and, on the other hand, the condition of 'Western' women is perceived as a clear evidence of the moral and civil decadence of the West. Such historical polemics continue and are sometimes reinforced, such as during the aftermath of 9/11 and the subsequent 'War on Terror', as part of the civilizational discourses and in a bid to increase the rhetorical arsenal. Yet, as we have observed in the previous chapters, if the literature concerning orientalism and the representation of Muslim women in the West have grown impressively, with tens of thousands of articles and thousands of books, studies on the representations of non-Muslim Western women among Muslims are greatly lacking. In other words, we will not find a book(s) similar to Kahf 's *Western Representations of the Muslim Woman: From Termagant to Odalisque* (1999) in English-language scholarly literature discussing the representations of Western women in Muslim-majority countries or among Muslim communities to this day. The reason for this gap in the literature is not clear; anyone who has travelled in the Middle East and to other Muslim countries knows that such representations do exist, just as they also exist among Muslim communities in the West. The lack of literature extends to historical times, since, for instance, while we have studies looking at the ideas that Europeans had of Ottoman women, we lack the opposite, despite the fact that there are Turkish documents and works that may shed light on the topic. In the following sections, I shall provide some examples of how 'civilizers' among both Muslims and Western non-Muslims use the rhetoric of gender in their struggles to civilize.

Veils, miniskirts, walking tents and uncovered meat: Saving women in the aftermath of September 11

In the now distant 1997, I was walking in Pisa when a rather odd billboard with an advertisement for stockings attracted my attention. It was not the standard picture of sexy legs that you may expect in such advertisements that caught my eye and caused me to stare at the billboard for a moment. Instead, I was surprised to see the image of four ladies, who were shrouded in a kind of black cloak from head to toe, raising their garment to the top of their sensual thighs. The punchline on the poster read, 'They cannot show them – you can', where 'them' referred not to the thighs but to the elaborate stockings. I was not yet an anthropologist and I did not spend much time analysing the message back then, yet the memory came back to me several years later at an airport in the UK, following the invasion of Afghanistan after 9/11. After a flight delay bestowed some unwanted free time upon me, I decided to perform the usual pilgrimage around the monotonous airport gadget shops and newsagents. While scanning some shelves filled with various magazines, the cover of a *National Geographic* issue attracted my attention.

A now-all-too familiar picture of a young woman with deep green eyes, exalted by the delicate frame of a red scarf, was, on the right-hand side, compared with a prematurely aged, unhealthy face which unemotionally surfaced from a deep blue burqa. The title on the cover emphatically announced, 'A Life Revealed'.[6] Although I needed some time to appreciate the similarity between the two faces, it was clear that the same woman owned both, though, indeed, diachronically.

The two portraits of the same woman seemingly wished to emphasize the degenerative effects that the Taliban's regime had on the young and beautiful woman who the photographer met for the first time in Afghanistan during the Russian occupation. 'Why such a cover?' I wondered. The answer could be found in a controversial conflict. The invasion of Afghanistan had until then failed in the task of capturing or killing Osama bin Laden – the Hindu Kush anchorman much loved by extremists worldwide – and had also missed the infamous one-eyed Mullah Omar. Yet, the US administration could still claim that something positive had come out of an unconvincing military campaign: they had freed Afghan women from the burqa, the quintessential symbol of 'Islamic' oppression. Much ink has been spent in magazines describing the oppression of Afghan women who were forced to wear the burqa, which had become, in the collective mass mediated unconscious, a symbol of Islam itself.

Anthropologist Jane Collier advanced the hypothesis that the image of 'oppressed' Muslim women played a role in the perception that Western women had reached higher levels of liberty in the 'civilised West' when compared to the 'barbaric East':

> Images of veiled Islamic women and walled harems must also have played a role in constructing understandings of Western women's liberties. It seems no accident, for example, that consent emerges as a key difference between 'oppressed' Islamic women and 'free' Western ones during the 19th century, when industrialization was transforming adult women from productive members of family enterprises into economic dependents of wage-earning husbands. ... Images of oppressed Islamic women, who could neither marry for love nor develop intimate relations with polygamous husbands, must have played a crucial role in constructing images of Western women as consenting to their disempowerment within increasingly privatized and confining homes. (Collier 1994: 407)

Definitely this dynamic has repeated itself and the Muslim woman has become again, particularly during the post-9/11 era, the obviously retrograde counterpoint of the Western woman who benefits from Western Judeo-Christian civilization. Muslim women in Afghanistan attracted the attention of the female partners of leaders such as Tony Blair and George Bush, so that, for example, Cherie Blair declared, 'Nothing more symbolises the oppression of women than the burqa, which is a very visible sign of the role of women in Afghanistan.'[7] Not dissimilarly, Laura Bush condemned the oppression of women in Afghanistan by stating that 'the fight against terrorism is also a fight for the rights and dignity of women' and 'civilized people throughout the world' (cited in Oliver 2013: 56). Laura Bush clearly supported the invasion, seeing it not only as a liberation programme but also as an operation that would prevent women in the West from possibly suffering one day the same conditions faced by women in Afghanistan and be deprived of their rights through the defeat of Western civilization: 'Civilized people throughout the world are speaking out in horror – not only because our hearts break for the women and children in Afghanistan, but also because in Afghanistan we see the world the terrorists would like to impose on the rest of us,' she proclaimed (Office of Mrs Bush 2001).

The focus on women's dress code and the civilizational discourse intensified with the invasion of Afghanistan, but they have a longer genealogy. In France, the long debate surrounding both the more common hijab (headscarf) and the quite rare burqa concluded in the French Senate on 14 September 2010, when a new controversial legislation banned any form of face-covering (such as the niqab) as well the burqa (Ismail 2010). Before this legislation, another one banned any visible religious symbol – which is not small enough to be concealed (like a small cross) – within the premises of public buildings. This legislation, introduced in 2004, appeared so clearly intended to target Muslim girls attending public schools that it was nicknamed the 'veil law' (Scott 2005). Other European countries moved to develop similar legislation. Feminists supported, as in the case of France, the ban of any veil since, as Elizabeth Badinter stated, 'the veil is a symbol of the oppression of a sex. Putting on torn jeans, wearing yellow, green or blue hair, this is an act of freedom with regards to the social conventions. Putting a veil on the head, this is an act of submission. It burdens a woman's whole life. Their fathers and their brothers choose their husbands, they are closed up in their own homes and confined to domestic tasks' (Cited in Malik 2010: 68). As Fernandez has suggested, the image of 'a weak and helpless woman who needs to be saved from barbaric customs and a brutal, all-powerful misogynistic group of men' is constantly deployed in discussions of Islam and its treatment of women, entrenching it deeper and more firmly in the public consciousness so that, in times of need, it can be called upon to justify whatever 'interventionist' measure is deemed necessary to save brown women from brown men (Fernandez 2009: 277).

Cooke has noticed the strong link between certain anti-veil positions and civilizational missions, where women are seen as in need of being rescued (i.e. taught how to be human) while the 'Other' men should be attacked and overcome: 'The men are the Other and the women are civilisable. To defend our universal civilisation we must rescue the women. To rescue these women we must attack these men. These women are to be rescued not because they are more "ours" than "theirs," but rather because they will have become more "ours" through the rescue mission.' (Cooke 2002: 227). Such rhetoric of salvation is nothing new. Indeed, as we have discussed in previous chapters, the genealogy of civilizers and the present clash of civilizers can be traced back to the long struggle between Manichean conceptualizations of a Christian West, ready through colonialism and religious missions to advance the backward and uncivilized Islamic world, and the Islamic world ready to bring the blessing of the 'peace' of Islam to the un-peacefully named geopolitical 'house of war' (dar-al-harb). Even some casual research reveals some historical pearls of this genealogy of intended salvation, so I will provide here only a few examples to illustrate. In Cairo, a conference for female Christian missionaries operating in the Arab World was organized, and in the conference proceedings we read, 'This book, with its sad reiterated story of wrong and oppression is an indictment and an appeal. ... It is an appeal to Christian womanhood to right these wrongs and enlighten this darkness by sacrifice and service. ... They will never cry for themselves, for they are down under the yoke of centuries of oppression' (von Sommer and Zwemmer 1907: 5, 15). The conference discussed veiling, forced marriages, polygamy and other aspects of women's lives in the Arab world, all of which, in the eyes of the Christian missionaries, demonstrated the oppression imposed by barbaric Muslim men and their religion.

The relationship between civilizational level and its observable signifiers has been often a matter of clothes and how much skin a woman is able to reveal in public. As Oliver correctly observes, 'Women's freedom in the West has been reduced to the freedom to dress … [and] to women's sexual freedom, which in turn is reduced to the freedom to reveal their bodies in public' (2013: 47, 51). He then concludes,

> In what ways do images of oppressed women elsewhere reassure Western women of their own freedom? … Certainly images from other countries where women appear completely covered, relegated to the domestic sphere, and denied freedom of expression make women in the West glad to live in a society that appears to value women's freedom. These images do seem to highlight the value placed on women's freedom in the West. (2013: 55)

The symbolic value of 'showing' or 'covering' the body has arrived at an unprecedented point of tension and I think it is not unreasonable to consider it one of the civilizers' weapons in the ongoing War on Terror, or in resistance to it. Recent developments include, for instance, the now well-known feminist group Femen, which formed in 2008 in Ukraine. Femen attracted international attention with their topless demonstrations (including in front mosques) and in August 2012 they staged a topless anti-Islamist protest in London at a time when the Olympics was being held. Another notable action has been the April 2013 Europe-wide 'topless jihad' protest in support of Tunisian activist Amina Tyler, who was arrested after posting tweets about the oppression of women in the Muslim world.[8] The issue at hand is not simply a campaign in support of women's rights but rather a proper 'civilizing' act against Islam – something which was confirmed by Femen's leader Inna Shevchenko on her Twitter feed on 9 July 2013, during the month of Ramadan, when she tweeted: 'What can be more stupid than Ramadan? What can be more villain than this religion [i.e. Islam]?' (cited in Timmerman 2013: 8).

The use of the body in demonstrations against Islam and sharia, in the name of rescuing Muslim women from what is perceived to be a barbaric androcentric religion, has expanded to include frequent displays of nudity, one of which was seen at the International Women's Day event, on 8 March 2014, when a group of female activists sported their birthday suits. Some activists present bore slogans in Arabic (some offensive to Muslim sensibilities) on their bodies and, in one case, the word Allah was removed from an Iranian flag – the part of the flag on which the word was written was torn – so that the circular hole seen could reveal the private parts of the naked protester behind it.[9] Mutatis mutandis, such use of the female body to provoke and upset religious Muslim men,[10] or at least the stereotype of them in the minds of the protesters, has the same rationale as that which made interrogators in the Abu Ghraib and Guantanamo Bay detention centres use female soldiers and their bodies as a means of torture against Arab prisoners – this point has been discussed by Oliver (2013: 20–45) and among others by Riley, Mohanty and Pratt (2008). The rhetorical weapons in the hands of 'Western' civilizers, which include condemnations against veiling, honour killings, underage religious marriages and, last but not least, female circumcision (better known as female genital mutilation), are decontextualized in their use, in particular on the internet, to convince non-Muslims in Western Europe (but increasingly also in Eastern Europe), the United States, Australia and New Zealand that Islam is not compatible with the West, which is seen as a signifier of civilization. It is not difficult to find numerous blogs, written by both conservative and progressive authors, pontificating that due to its treatment of women, Islam (or for the moderate commentators 'some aspects of Islam') has little space in 'civilized' countries.

For instance, a small event, organized by a rather controversial Muslim group at the University of Melbourne, in which students were invited to sit in sex-segregated areas, with women seated at the back of the room, sparked a national debate. The reaction was heated and newspapers covered the controversy with articles such as 'Academic calls for end to ritualised humiliation',[11] 'Abbott condemns Melbourne University over sex segregation at Islamic events'[12] and 'Melbourne's hypocrisy on gender naive'.[13] Most of the arguments presented centred around a presumption that sex segregation is against Australian values and humiliates women. The rhetoric appeared to have a paternalist tone since no Muslim woman at the event was interviewed or otherwise given an opportunity to voice her opinion. It was implied that there was only one correct way to be a woman, and that way was the Australian, and by extension 'Western', way (as conceptualized by each author).

Is this focus on Muslim women's dress code solely the result of Islamophobic media and anti-Muslim sentiments? Although many studies seem to suggest so,[14] I have noticed that often the processes by which mass media stereotypes are developed are better understood as dynamics. In this case, it is easy to see that most of the negative focus on Muslim veils is an internal debate within European and other Western countries. Yet, we also have to notice that much of the Muslim debate about headscarves or more conservative Muslim women's dress codes are also within Muslim communities living in Western countries. After 11 September and during the War on Terror, strong positions about the 'modesty' of women, demonstrated through the wearing of hijab or other forms of veiling, have been expressed within Muslim communities. For example, in 2008, I was told in a Scottish mosque that 'a Muslim woman who does not wear the hijab is not a real Muslimah', and when I asked why this was so, the imam explained that things had changed: 'There was more tolerance for this behaviour when I was young. Today it is different –you must show that you are a Muslim woman, that you are modest, since you must be different from the western woman. I mean, the veil clarifies this difference. It is essential since Muslim women are the guardians of Islam.'

The above point was confirmed in a discussion with an Australian imam I met. He said:

> You are right, the hijab is not a pillar of Islam. But it is important that our women show modesty and are different from the Australian non-Muslims. We need that our daughters see their mother to be modest; this is the best example to protect them from the *kafir* (unbelieving) environment they live in. I think the community is right to put a bit of pressure to educate the sisters that still do not cover properly.

Although many Muslim women dress religiously because they want to express their faith, an increasing number adopt the veil not just as an act of spirituality but also as a political statement. Even more numerous are the Muslim men who interpret Muslim women's veils as a political statement. Many in European and Australian Muslim communities, indeed, perceive the decision not to wear a veil as a form of Westernization. As Sharif explained in the London mosque where I was visiting, 'Today Muslim women do not wear the hijab or fear wearing a niqab because they have westernised. They think that integration and acceptance is more important than *iman* (faith), so they give in to *dunia* [the material world].' It is not surprising that non-Muslim women, who are referred to by an increasing number of Muslims in the West as 'kafir', are the symbols of the decadence of Christianity and Western civilization.

It is not difficult to find evidence of an increased effort after 9/11 that aims to 'save' non-Muslim women from the decadent culture of the West. The rhetoric of these civilizers is a mirror image of the one we have just discussed. For instance, Sheik Taj el-Din al-Hilali, a top cleric in the Sydney Muslim community, stated during a Ramadan sermon in 2006 that was attended by more than 500 worshipers,

> If you take out uncovered meat and place it outside on the street, or in the garden or in the park, or in the backyard without a cover, and the cats come and eat it ... whose fault is it, the cats or the uncovered meat? ...The uncovered meat is the problem. If she was in her room, in her home, in her hijab, no problem would have occurred.[15]

The statement attracted the attention of the media since it was uttered in defence of a recently sentenced group of rapists. The sheik apologized and asserted that he was only 'defending the honour of women'. Yet, what Sheik Taj el-Din al-Hilali expressed that day, in front of 500 Muslim worshipers, was exactly what a significant number wanted to hear. He paid publicly for expressing what many Muslims, both living in the West and in Muslim-majority countries, think. His statement that he was actually protecting the honour of women is equivalent to the statements that we have read above, in which the ban of the burqa, niqab or the hijab is proposed or advocated in the name of the 'dignity' of women.

When I have discussed this well-known controversy with Muslims living in Australia, the positions are, of course, varied. Jamila, a 22-year-old undergraduate student at a local university, had this to say:

> The comments were insensitive. How would the victims of those rapes feel? I can only imagine. However, he [Sheik Taj el-Din al-Hilali] was speaking to Muslims during a sermon and not to the general public or on television. I have to say that I agree that, in Australia, women do not dress to protect their honour and it is a concern for Muslim families since our sisters are exposed to western culture that lacks modesty. The words were strong, but not false. He stated a fact.

The Muslim men I discussed the same controversy with seemed often ready to justify the sheik's position; for instance, Yusuf, a community worker in Western Sydney, expressed in clear words:

> Western culture. They do whatever they want. Have you been to King's Cross yet? Go and see Satan in action. All those naked women. They are agents of Satan. You do not know where to look, even during the day! Western women have no morals and create what the Sheik was speaking about. They provoke men, the bringing them towards Satan. Western culture is full of it, and Muslims will be protected from temptations only if Sharia is, insha'Allah, implemented.

One aspect of the civilizing rhetoric we can encounter among Muslims is the idea that Western women are oppressed by their own culture. Asma, working as teacher in a Western Sydney public school, stated,

> We all know who the oppressed women are in this world. It's not the Muslim women but the non-Muslims – since you cannot deny the pressure that they have to maintain a certain weight, standard of dress and make-up and they spend all their energy trying to look beautiful. A Muslim woman does

not need this. Islam freed them from this pettiness. Islam is the solution for the happiness of women and indeed many Australian women are reverting to Islam, masha'Allah! The Western culture is the most oppressive of all. Islam is the solution. Insha'Allah more and more Australians will see the practicality of Allah's divine guidance every day.

The list of societal practices mentioned to me to demonstrate that 'Western culture' and 'Western values' are uncivilized and negatively affect women is quite long and the implication was often that Islam is the realistic possibility for their rescue. Abdullah, a second-generation Lebanese man who works at a local gym, provided some examples from this list:

> Western countries, like Australia, authorise pornography, multiple sexual partners, brothels and all this western sexual liberation which truthfully affects women, enslaves women and does not protect them. It exploits them. The glorification of fornication within western culture is at such an obscene level that it is unparalleled in any other culture. The reason is that in the West, like in Australia, people are entitled to have individual rights – like to do whatever they want and so the law cannot protect women, or children. Instead the law of God, the Sharia, is universal and gives women real freedom to be how God wanted them to be. And also men can be protected from lust and all the horrible things Muslims must see in this country.

The idea that 'Western values' demonstrate a lack of real civilization is even stronger in Muslim-majority countries from the Middle East, South Asia and Southeast Asia. Westernization is a strongly negative label, similarly to how 'Islamization' is for a great number of people in Europe and other Western countries. Again, in Malaysia, Indonesia and even among Muslims in Singapore, it is women and sexual behaviours or women's dress choices in particular that are used as a basis to show that the 'West' is immoral and Islam (or sharia in other cases) is the only remedy.

Saving Islam from gays, saving gays from Islam

We have seen how the discourse of saving 'Muslim women' from brown Muslim men (Abu-Lughod 2002, 2013) has been central to the aim of civilizers to 'educate' Muslim women on how to be women. Indeed, Abu-Lughod recently observes that 'gendered orientalism has taken on a new life and new forms in our feminist twenty first century' (2013: 202). We have also observed a mirroring discourse of saving women from a perceived degenerate and immoral 'West'. Yet, this is not the only gender dynamic in which civilizers are interested. A new area of confrontation has developed. Since the 1980s, Western countries and their governments have moved a long way in the effort to acknowledge the civil and legal rights of non-heterosexuals (Marcus 2002). This has brought about conditions that enabled the recent campaign for 'gay marriages' to achieve clear results in the UK and several US states, despite strong resistance and controversies.[16]

The LGBT movement has globalized, and interest in the lives, difficulties and challenges of non-Western non-heterosexuals has increased in the new millennium – this has included campaigns for the rights of gays and lesbians in the Middle East and in the Muslim world. Blogs, newspaper articles, TV programmes, documentaries, films[17] and novels (Abraham 2008) have described the ostracism, fear and risks that non-heterosexual individuals living in Muslim majority countries often face. All this Western attention on Muslim LGBTs in Muslim majority countries has in reality increased the pressure on such individuals. Indeed, several Arab governments, as well as the Iranian government, seem to have increased the intensity of their persecution and, in the case of Iran, this has meant an increasing number of executions of gay activists.

The globalized debate about 'gay rights' has also provoked reactions among Muslims in Asia. In Singapore, for example, although the debate about homosexuality existed within the local Muslim communities, Muslims did not tend to openly oppose non-heterosexuals who made their sexual preferences publicly known. Yet, concerns about homosexuality among the Malay community have increased ever since Singaporean society began to show a secular tolerance towards homosexuality, this being seen, for instance, in the annual organization of Pink Dot.[18] The resulting anti-homosexuality activism has not been devoid of controversy. For instance, an associate professor at the National University of Singapore's Department of Malay Studies, Syed Muhd Khairudin Aljunied, was forced to apologize and delete a Facebook post that likened lesbians to 'cancers' that must be stopped 'in their tracks'. The main concern expressed by the associate professor was that such 'ideology' threatened to corrupt Islam since the homosexual way of life would 'spread like wild fire'; he concluded his post saying, 'All diseases must end at home. ... Together, we will stop these cancers in their tracks!'[19]

Associate Professor Syed Muhd Khairudin Aljunied was reprimanded for expressing publicly on a social network what many Muslims agree with in silence or only discuss in 'safe' places, such as after Friday prayers and among friends. Yet, the associate professor has been clearly misunderstood. Instead of speaking about gays and lesbians in general, he was speaking about a fear.

This fear, as we shall see, is linked to what Prof Aljunied often identifies as 'liberal Islam' in his public posts. We have seen in previous chapters how 'liberal Islam' is identified by a large number of Muslims to be a Western invention to weaken Islam; or in other words, to make Islam Westernized. The 'cancer' in this case is not the individual person who is gay or lesbian, but rather the perceived attack against the 'correct' way of being human. The discussion about liberal Islam and the opposition to it is linked to the effects of the 11 September aftermath. Far from being innocent, liberal Islam is perceived as a weapon that can strike from within and 'uncivilize' Islam.

Many Muslims also link 'liberal Islam' to the risk of an increase of homosexuality among Muslims, since the perception that homosexuality is a Western disease is one of the most common statements. Abbul, a 28-year-old Palestinian living in Sydney, observed, 'The issue with homos is that they corrupt society. Now we live here in Australia, and our children are at a risk. It is a western illness and something they [the children] can learn from here. Yes, we may have some homos in the Middle East, but they do not show their homosexuality in public. It is an issue of visibility.' The fact that Western countries no longer have specific laws to punish homosexuality, and instead have legislation that protects it as part of individual freedom, as well as events such as Mardi Gras or Gay Pride parades, become the evidence that a gay agenda exists (Sanjakdar 2013). In a closed online Muslim forum, Abdul makes exactly this point when he writes, 'Homosexuality was a crime a few years ago and now it's a fashion. This is just another symptom of the problem of secular society. We have the so-called personal freedoms but when members of the society accept these ideas of personal freedoms, then we see such behaviour i.e. homosexuality.'

While Muslim majority countries are introducing more restrictive legislation against homosexuality,[20] Muslim communities in the West find themselves living in societies that are fast approaching the total normalization of non-heterosexual life, where same-sex attracted people are allowed to marry or adopt children as couples and are visible in the media in advertisements and TV programmes. Even more challenging is dealing with the education that their Muslim children may be exposed to: a secular education that may teach them that to be homosexual is not a sin, which, of course, contradicts what they are taught at the mosque and at home. Such contradiction is well explained by Jasmine, a 35-year-old Muslim social worker who lives in Glasgow,

> I think we need to respect everybody as a person, as indeed Islam teaches. Yet, how can I accept that my children are exposed to ideas that contradict not just religion but also how to be a good human being loved by Allah. At the end, Muslims should learn to submit to Allah. The West teaches you

that you are totally free. The problem is here in the understanding of how to be men and women, how be what Allah wants us to be.

In her study, Sanjakdar (2013) has shown some examples of Muslim teachers' views concerning 'how homosexuality should be discussed with their Muslim students and more broadly with Muslim youth living in the West' (2013: 17). She shows how the Muslim teachers understood homosexuality as something learnt and of course that 'the issue of a homosexual Muslim is "nonsense" and "non-existent" in Islam'. (Sanjakdar 2013: 23)

In a study on queer Muslims in Australia, one of Abraham's respondents observes that 'the concept of orientation comes from the West [and] the idea of Western identity is rejected, so too is the notion of sexual orientation, which comes to be viewed as "just a choice for hedonism"' (Abraham 2009: 85). The link between hedonism and the Western way of life is, as we have seen in the previous chapters, a recurring topic in the rhetoric of would-be Muslim civilizers, for whom Islam is often reduced to a religion of abstinence, honour, sacrifice (if not martyrdom) and courage, while forgetting all the other elements of Islam which focus on living one's life in peace and happiness. Indeed, as Belk et al. have observed, hedonism is more accepted in Islam and less of a sin than in Christianity because Islam permits the pursuit of happiness and desires as long as they lie within the boundaries of what is moral and just. Civilizers among Muslims, however, have normally a somewhat puritanical view of Islam, just like the view that the civilizers among the conservative members of the different churches of Christianity have of their religion (see, for instance, Maddox 2003).

If on one side of the coin is the narrative that Islam must be protected from a perceived widespread 'gay agenda' of the West as well as so-called Westernizing attempts, the other side of the coin is the increased presence in Western countries of new '"rescue gays" narratives in ways that bring to mind the previously discussed "rescue women" scripts' (Bracke 2012: 245). For instance, people who oppose Islam in Australia and what they see as the 'danger' of sharia, express what, according to them, would happen to non-heterosexuals if Muslims had their own way: 'They throw gays down a cliff! If you read some of their forums, they say things like we must throw them off buildings! That shows us what kind of people they are. Islam is a barbaric cult, full stop.' This was written in an online conversation by a very concerned member of a FB group aimed at stopping sharia in Australia. Another member of the same group added that, although Christians have their problems with gays and hold conservative opinions about homosexuality,

Muslims are a danger to our free society because they do not value personal freedom, so they do not respect gays. They say horrible things, like that we are immoral, that we are evil and corrupt. Christianity is changing, but Muslims have a very violent way of expressing themselves against gays that shows that they have yet to be integrated in this society.

This point was reinforced by an additional member, who wrote, 'Islam and Muslims are a serious threat to the life of gay people. If they had their way and implemented Shari'a in our country, lots of people would be killed.'

Politicians, in particular from the political right, have expressed, for instance in the Netherlands (Aydemir 2012; Jivraj and De Jong 2011), what they believe to be the risk that Islam and Muslims may pose towards the LGBT community. For example on 11 May 2002, the Dutch prime minister during his weekly ten-minute interview spent time exhorting Muslims to respect Dutch tolerance of homosexuality (reported in Hekma 2002: 242). Mepschen, Duyvendak and Tonkens (2010) have suggested that such interest in sexuality among politicians, many of whom have never been particularly supportive of non-heterosexual identities, is in reality part of an anti-Muslim discourse. For instance, former Dutch politician Pim Fortuyn adopted the image of the 'liberated gay man' (Van der Veer 2006), whose freedom and gay identity was threatened in the Netherlands even before Muslims took interest in him. Mepschen et al. argues that the sexual orientalism employed was effective in presenting sexual liberation as an expression of modern, secular Dutchness and as a means of highlighting the perceived backwardness of Muslims (Mepschen, Duyvendak and Tonkens 2010: 970). Yet, Mepschen has identified an important contradiction in the very vocal criticisms of Islam and Muslims that often come from feminist and gay right activists as well as politicians:

In order to criticize Muslims as backwards and as enemies of European culture, gay rights are now heralded as if they have been the foundation of European culture for centuries (cf. Wekker: 2009). This instrumentalization of gay rights puts progressives, anti-racists, feminists, and lesbian and gay activists in an impossible position: taking up the defence of lesbian and gay rights and public gayness comes to be associated with Islamophobia, while solidarity with Muslims against Islamophobia is represented, especially by the populist right, as trivializing or even supporting 'Muslim' homophobia. (2010: 965)

Nonetheless, the contradiction is not resolved, since, as we have discussed, at stake is 'a temporal narrative framing European modernity against Muslim tradition, where sexual freedom has come to stand, metonymically, for secularism and rational, liberal subjectivity' (Mepschen, Duyvendak and Tonkens 2010: 964). Indeed, homophobia, as it has been named in the West, is not a Muslim problem. If, for instance, we consider that Muslims in, for example, the United Kingdom, Australia, and even the United States (just to name some countries) comprise a tiny fraction of the overall population,[21] the impact compared to the overall population is surely extremely limited, and the attention to such a tiny population of residents and citizens appears rather disproportional when compared to the presence of homophobia among right-wing parties and extreme Fascist movements or even some Christian sects.

Bracke, in an article titled 'From "saving women" to "saving gays": Rescue narratives and their dis/continuities', provides a convincing argument that the rhetoric of saving gays from Muslims is a parallel version of saving Muslim women from Muslim men and it is part of a 'civilizing mission' (2012: 241). Bracke, however, has observed that the two 'rescue' narratives function differently. According to him, the first difference 'pertains to the *subject of rescue*' since 'brown women need to shed off their damaging cultural and religious attachments in order for them to be emancipated, and if it's not brown men hindering them to do so, then it might be their own "false consciousness"' (2012: 247, italics in the original), while for the brown gays (i.e. Muslims) false consciousness plays a minor role compared to the subjectivity and specific understandings of coming out. In other words, it is the action of 'coming out' that saves the gay Muslim from his own religion and makes him part of the secular civil West. The second point, Bracke has observed, is that the narrative of civilizational homosexuality, which during the colonial times was used to demonize Muslim men as weak and effeminate when compared to the 'white' strong and civilized men (Haritaworn, Tauqir and Erdem 2008; Puar 2007), has turned on itself, with homosexuality now epitomizing tolerance, which we have observed in this book is one of the most emphasized 'tools' of western civilization to demonstrate the barbaric other. Indeed, if 'the moral' and 'just' are the main arguments of the Muslim civilizer, 'tolerance', 'gender equality' and 'freedom' are those of the Judeo-Christian one.

They are taking our women away!

Legend has it that the Romans, lacking women of their own, decided in 750 BCE to *raptio* women from the neighbouring group, the Sabines. This became known as the 'rape of the Sabine women', which would be better translated from the Latin as 'the abduction of the Sabine women' (Feldherr 2009: 280–89). The fear that foreigners may take women from local men is not a new one; if you add Islam to the equation, we can find legends and real stories which go back centuries, as in the well-worn trope of the Muslim corsairs kidnapping women in order to refurnish a sultan's harem (Hoeveler 2006; Shaheen 2000). At the same time, Muslims have, in particular when living in Western countries, expressed concerns that Western culture may 'take' their daughters away from the right path, both in religious and cultural terms. It is no surprise, then, that this trope is exploited by those whom we have identified in this book as 'civilizers'.

During the years of the War on Terror, what was before a mere voice rose to become a call of alarm. This period heralded an increasing number of frequently alarmist mass media reports suggesting that Muslims were taking white women again, although this time they were not strangers coming from the sea. Settled as they were within local urban landscapes, these Muslims did not come from a distant land; they were instead an integral part of British society. The police in the UK also started to speak of Muslims, in particular Asian Muslims, as involved in grooming young, vulnerable white teenagers for sex or prostitution and as sex gang predators.[22] It was not just notorious anti-Muslim websites such as *Jihad Watch*[23] that reinforced fears; the mass media ran headlines such as 'Special investigation: how predatory gangs force middle-class girls into the sex trade',[24] 'I was kept prisoner by the Asian sex gang predator: victim tells harrowing story of "boyfriend" who dubbed his car the "Rape Rover"'[25] and politicians made statements showing that they were ready to act. Former secretary Jack Straw upset the Pakistani Muslim community when he stated the following on 9 January 2011:

> These young men are in a western society, in any event, they act like any other young men, they're fizzing and popping with testosterone, they want some outlet for that, but Pakistani heritage girls are off-limits and they are expected to marry a Pakistani girl from Pakistan, typically. ... So they then seek other avenues and they see these young women, white girls who are vulnerable, some of them in care ... who they think are easy meat. ... And because they're vulnerable they ply them with gifts, they give them drugs, and then of course they're trapped.[26]

Although, as we have seen in this chapter, a certain problematic narrative about non-Muslim white women exists in the Muslim community, Jack Straw's patronizing words laid blame on an entire community. His choice of words, which highlighted how the men were living in a Western society, appeared to imply that these young Asian Muslims were not used to the freedom that Western civilization provided. Straw completely overlooked the fact that the culprits in the few criminal cases were not migrants but third-generation Muslims, more British than Pakistani; limited opportunities to date or marry Pakistani girls and local realities had little to do, as my research in UK prisons also demonstrates (Marranci 2009), with the focused targeting of white non-Muslim girls. The mass media ignored, furthermore, that a number of South Asian girls, most of whom – like their white counterparts – were drug abusers, had been introduced to prostitution via the same criminal circuit. Cockbain, author of one of the few studies focusing on this issue, has observed,

The image of the Asian groomer has proved a seductive and enduring one, yet, as this article has demonstrated, the idea of a uniquely Asian crime threat is ill founded, misleading and dangerous. The construction of grooming as a distinct offence and a racial crime threat has been shown to lie on insubstantial foundations: misconceptions, anecdote, opinion and the deliberate manipulation of limited statistics of dubious provenance. (2013: 30)

In Australia, the convictions for sexual assault of up to fourteen young teenagers of Lebanese Muslim background in Sydney during the 2000 Olympic Games has, like in the UK, provoked the stereotype of the Muslims 'hunting' white Australian girls (Gleeson 2004). Although a racist and anti-Western motive for the crime can be easily deduced from the accounts of the victims and how the perpetrators behaved in court, the consequent rhetoric of Muslim-hatred and the implication that Islam was behind the behaviour of the culprits (Poynting et al. 2004) revealed a civilizational discourse, which became even more apparent during the so-called Cronulla Riots that took place in the Sydney suburb of Cronulla in December 2005 (Poynting 2006). The conflict again derived from the tensions between some white non-Muslim Australians complaining about the behaviour of some Lebanese working class youth towards white women. A strong campaign organized by right wing movements provoked the riots in which the notion of 'barbaric' Muslims, who need to be expelled, was evident.

Most academics researching Muslim communities in the West have not focused on this civilizational discourse, and indeed the work of Cockbain (2013) is at present the only traceable academic article that discusses it. The links seen in this discourse between gender, race and Islam are unprecedented, a product clearly of the narrative of fear derived from the War on Terror. For instance, after the Cronulla Riots, local politician Bruce Baird explained the riots as a consequence of the rapes and terrorism: 'I can understand at one level at people's frustration because they all feel that the beaches belong to them and it is a Sutherland Shire thing and when anybody disturbs the equilibrium, given all the events that have happened since September 11, I just think that's the match that sets alight the fuel.'[27] The tensions between Muslim and non-Muslim communities have increased as have the number of those who feel they have the right to 'teach' others how to be a civilized human. In the case of women, this may lead to some of them paying the ultimate price, as in the case of what has been called 'honour killings', an issue that has now attracted particular attention (Mosquera 2013).

On the one hand, again, something that is a very rare occurrence among certain ethnic groups has been transformed into yet more evidence of not only incompatibility with Western life of the entire population of those who identify their beliefs with Islam, but also of the barbarism of the latter (Mirza 2013a, b).

In a piece titled, 'Twisted concept of honour shames any civilised society',[28] Ruth Dudley Edwards, an Irish historian, speaks of 'domestic terrorism' and asks how a civilized society may accept such cultural norms. On the other hand, however, some Muslim women are victims of civilizational discourses within their own families. Indeed, a review of the known reasons for 'honour killings' committed in Anglo-Saxon countries appears to suggest a majority concern accusations, in one form or another, of Westernization (Chestler 2010: 5).

During my research on Muslim prisoners in the UK (Marranci 2009), I interviewed a Kurdish man who killed his daughter in 2003 because she moved in with her boyfriend, who was not Muslim. During the interview, the sentenced father showed great remorse about the actual killing, but yet did not see his actions as being immoral. The reason for such contradiction was to be found in the idea of his daughter being 'too Westernized', as she was dressing, speaking and acting as an ordinary British girl instead of as a Muslim Kurd. The father was left feeling that he had no choice but to demonstrate to his Kurdish community that he had 'honour' and could control his children. Indeed, in that act of killing his daughter, the father was in reality killing the 'West' that he saw as the ultimate Satan. Killing the daughter was also intended to provide an example to other children: a desperate act to transform her into the human being that she ought to be, even if this meant taking her life. She was now a martyr, as he clearly explained, 'I deserve to die and I have stated so in court, asking for the death penalty, so that then through my punishment I can clean my sins. Yet I saved my daughter since by killing her I made her a martyr and I will be punished by Allah, who however is the most merciful.'

Although statistics concerning violence related to the concept of honour are scarce and fragmented since they are also controversial, a recent report in December 2011 from the UK Police provided some partial numbers, derived from the records kept by 32 out of 59 police forces, as a result of a 'freedom of information' request made by the Iranian and Kurdish Women's Rights Organisation (Ikwro). This report revealed what the Ikwro identified as 2,823 'honour related attacks'.[29] Of cases that occurred in a Western country, most perpetrators adduced Westernization or Westernized behaviour as provoking the violence.

Conclusion

Civilization narratives have always included discussions of the treatment of women. Although often perceived as the backbones of cultural transmission and as protectors of tradition, women are sometimes also seen as making vulnerable the same traditions they teach to new generations. In the aftermath of 11 September and the continuing War on Terror, women have found themselves not only on the battlefield as fighters (Oliver 2013) or as part of a resistance (Von Knop 2007), protesting against the war or defending the rights of their children and people (Rashid 2013), but also as part of civilizational narratives, often discussed and argued by men. Furthermore, recent narratives of gender and civilization have extended to non-heterosexuals. Although Muslim and non-Muslim civilizers often express two opposing arguments, the differing arguments both derive from the same ideology: the idea that there is only one way to be a proper human.

This produces, in the case of gender, the two dynamics that we have observed in this chapter. The first is the parallel arguments aimed at dehumanizing the other through the essentialization of culture and gender. Western narratives that are aimed at presenting Islam and Muslims as uncivilized have focused on the condition of women in Islam. Of course, these narratives are selective and based, as we have observed, on stereotypes where women are represented as oppressed, weak and vulnerable. Among the most mentioned supposed demonstrations of such oppressive reality is the Islamic dress code: the veil in its various traditional varieties. It is interesting here to mention that many Muslim men, even living in the West, adopt Islamic styles of appearance and attire, such as a beard and, in some cases, traditional clothes. Despite this, most of the discussion focuses on women and practically never on men; this is also despite the fact that, for instance, in Afghanistan the dress code rules for men were no less oppressive than those for women and many Afghan men happily shaved their imposed Pashtun style beards after Kabul was freed from the Taliban and swapped their long robes for blue jeans (Fowler 2007). Real issues such as female genital mutilation, honour-related violence and the restriction of movement for women are manipulated to demonstrate the superiority of Western culture and the right to impose it, even through wars of dubious legality. However, at the same time, Muslim civilizers also have their arsenal of stereotypes and narratives. As we have seen, such stereotypes focus on the lack of morality and dignity of the West. Again, women are the main protagonists, the difference being that the focus is on the miniskirt instead of the burqa. The second dynamic is the mission to 'save' people. Women, and as we have observed non-heterosexuals, need to be rescued by Islam and sharia or by secularism and democracy.

As multiculturalism is challenged and questioned in this post-September 11 context (Kuo 2013; Poynting 2013; Modood 2013) by mass media, politicians and ordinary people, the civilizing rhetoric is reinforced and with it are the aspects that we have discussed in this chapter. Values enter the stage and often the clash is of symbols: the rejection and attack on the veil or the miniskirt becomes essential elements of dehumanizing the other. The real condition of women, as well as the real treatment of non-heterosexuals has, even historically, never ontologically interested civilizers. Instead, such discourse has an easily accessible emotional appeal that can attract and convince those in the civilizing mission, normally a majority, who are not fully committed to such an effort. The call for 'saving', 'protecting', 'educating' and 'freeing' women and non-heterosexuals from Islam, or similarly rescuing Muslims and Islam from perceived Western deviances, may work as a powerful cognitive opening to facilitate the spread of the civilizational idea. And, indeed, I think today we have strong examples of the success that such rhetoric can achieve in increasing divisions, tensions and conflicts between Muslims and non-Muslims.

Notes

1   The first part of the title is derived from a blog post by Sayantani DasGupta, http://www.racialicious.com/2012/10/08/your-women-are-oppressed-but-ours-are-awesome-how-nicholas-kristof-and-half-the-sky-use-women-against-each-other/ (accessed 1 May 2014).

2   It was painted outside his glass workshop in 2010, http://www.dailytelegraph.com.au/ban-the-burqa-mural-not-anti-muslim-says-artist/story-e6freuy9-1225928451622 (accessed 1 May 2014).

3   https://www.facebook.com/pages/Ban-The-Burka-in-Australia/143853875636952 (accessed 1 May 2014).

4   http://www.australiandefenceleague.com.au/v2.0/ and http://www. http://sheikyermami.com/ (both accessed 1 May 2014).

5   Of course, as we shall discuss, today the reality is reversed and women's emancipation and participation in politics is one of the main 'litmus tests' to evaluate the civilizational level of a nation or society.

6   A photo of the cover can be seen at http://s.ngm.com/afghan-girl/images/afghan-girl.jpg (accessed 1 May 2014).

7   Independent, 20 November 2001.

8   http://www.theatlantic.com/infocus/2013/04/femen-stages-a-topless-jihad/100487/ (accessed 1 May 2014).

9   For more information and an explanation of the event, please refer to the activists' blog: http://freethoughtblogs.com/maryamnamazie/2014/03/08/nude-protest-for-intl-womens-day/ (accessed 1 May 2014).

10   The main target, indeed, since the religious women are the ones to be saved.

11   Rachel Baxendale, The Australian 26 April 2013, http://www.theaustralian.com.au/higher-education/academic-calls-for-end-to-ritualised-humiliation/story-e6frgcjx-1226629597535# (accessed 1 May 2014).

12   Ben Packman, The Australian 26 April 2013, http://www.theaustralian.com.au/national-affairs/abbott-condemns-melbourne-university-over-sex-segregation-at-islamic-events/story-fn59niix-1226630024655# (accessed 1 May 2014).

13 Dr Jennifer Oriel, News. Com 26 April 2013, http://www.news. com.au/national/melbournes-hypocrisy-on-gender-naive/story-e6frfkp9-1226630187844 (accessed 1 May 2014).

14 See, for instance, among the recent literature: Navarro (2010), Williamson and Khiabany (2010), Eltantawy (2013) and Mirza (2013a, b).

15 http://www.cbsnews.com/news/muslim-cleric-calls-women-uncovered-meat/ (accessed 1 May 2014).

16 See the recent resignation of Mozilla CEO over a donation to an anti-gay marriage group: http://www.theguardian.com/technology/2014/apr/03/mozilla-ceo-brendan-eich-resigns-prop-8 (accessed 1 May 2014).

17 See, for instance, the film 'A Jihad for Love' by Parvez Sharma. For a review of the film, please see Bao (2013).

18 Pink Dot SG is an annual, non-profit movement and an event that started in 2009 in support of the Lesbian, Gay, Bisexual and Transgender community in Singapore; for more information, see http://pinkdot.sg/ (accessed 1 May 2014).

19 https://sg.news.yahoo.com/nus-professor-controversially-likens-lesbianism-to-cancer-sparks-protest-letter-from-graduates-014042548.html (accessed 1 May 2014).

20 'Straight but Narrow; Islam and Homosexuality.' The Economist 402.870 (2012): 63–64.

21 Pew Research (2011), Muslim Population, http://features.pewforum.org/muslim-population/ (accessed 1 May 2014).

22 See, for instance, The Times, 'Barnardo's demands inquiry into sex exploitation of British girls', published online (5 January 2011), http://www.thetimes.co.uk/tto/news uk/crime/arti- cle2864090.ece (accessed 1 May 2014).

23 Jihad Watch is a well-known and popular website hosted by Robert Spencer that is aimed at alerting people to what he perceives as the danger of Islam to Western societies.

24 Daily Mail, 'Special investigation: how predatory gangs force middle-class girls into the sex trade', published online (7 July 2010), http://www.dailymail.co.uk/news/article- 1301003/Special-investigation-How-predatory-gangs-force-middle-class-girls-sex-trade.html (accessed 1 May 2014).

25 Daily Mail, 'I was kept prisoner by the Asian sex gang predator: victim tells harrowing story of "boyfriend" who dubbed his car the "Rape Rover"', published online (5 January 2011), http://www.dailymail.co.uk/news/article-1347335/Asian-sex-ganToni-Marie-Redferns- boyfriend-dubbed-car-Rape-Rover.html (accessed 1 May 2014).

26 Excerpt from Batty (2011). 'White girls seen as "easy meat" by Pakistani rapists, says Jack Straw'. The Guardian, 8 January 2011, http://www.theguardian.com/world/2011/jan/08/jack-straw-white-girls-easy-meat (accessed 1 May 2014).

27 AAP. (2005), 'Terrorism, Gang Rapes Behind Riots': MP. 12 December, http://www.smh.com.au/news/national/terrorism-gang-rapes-behind-riots-mp/2005/12/12/1134235978344.html (accessed 1 May 2014).

28 Dudley Edwards, The Independent Ireland, 1 December 2012, http://www.independent.ie/opinion/columnists/ruth-dudley-edwards/ruth-dudley-edwards-twisted-concept-of-honour-shames-any-civilised-society-26818391.html (accessed 1 May 2014).

29 See BBC Online 'Honour' attack numbers revealed by UK police forces', http://www.bbc.com/news/uk-16014368 (accessed 1 May 2014).

6

Drones, jihad and justice

Alhamdulillah! Our brother is a martyr, more Australian Muslims
should follow the beautiful path towards paradise.
Muslims will finally have their khalifate; Jihad will prevail.
My brothers, come to Jihad!

It is not difficult to navigate in Facebook pages, Twitter accounts and other social media (from Tumblr to Instagram) to find words in support of ISIS (Islamic State in Iraq and the Levant, today known as the Islamic State), the Islamic insurgency movement in Syria and Iraq. There is an excitement among certain Muslim groups and individuals; as Ahmad (a 25-year-old student of Lebanese background) observed,

> There is the feeling that what is happening is very different from al-Qaeda times. There is a certain awareness that groups such as ISIS or even Boko Harãm want to fight for an Islamic state, and not just fight for the sake of fighting as al-Qaeda has done for too long.
> The idea is that finally an Islamic state based on Shari'a without any compromise, a state made of mujahideen and built through the blessed blood of martyrs will finally bring back the splendour of Islam and justice for Muslims; all Muslims.

An increasing number of Western-born Muslims and, in particular, converts are leaving their countries to join revolutionary Islamic groups, such as ISIS, which currently appears to be the most violent, ruthless and unstoppable of them. Newspapers speak of 150 or even 200 in Australia,[1] and recent estimates suggest that the same Islamic organization has recruited up to 1,500 British Muslims (and probably this is a conservative estimate).[2] Similarly, in Germany,

France, Italy and the United States, young Muslims from different ethnic, social and economic backgrounds have left their country to join the 'Jihad'.

The decision is not without consequences. Not only do they run the risk of being killed (yet a considerable number of fellow Muslims will see them as martyrs), but they also run the risk of seeing their passport cancelled and even their citizenship questioned.[3] Yet, as Aakif in a Muslim forum said, 'If they are blessed with martyrdom, they do not need to come back to the land of the Australian Kafirun since the Khalifate will be established in the Middle East.' The confidence in the establishment of the new Islamic state is very high also among Muslims who do not directly condone indiscriminate acts of violence such as those perpetrated by ISIS. In this chapter we will see why the concept of jihad, as I have defined elsewhere, is 'beyond Islam' (Marranci 2006), and has become even more attractive than during the period immediately after 9/11 and the ensuing conflict in Afghanistan and Iraq.

The term 'jihad' can be understood in many ways depending upon many variables: the context in which it is used, who is employing it, the place where it is discussed and the reasons for which it is mentioned (Marranci 2006; Cook 2005; Bonney 2004). Yet in this chapter, we are not dealing with the 'theological' concept or even the 'politically correct' usage, but rather with a concept that is derived from a specific view of Islam which exists among some Muslims. Indeed, during my study of the rhetoric of jihad among European Muslims, I concluded that some Muslims 'do not speak of and act for "jihad" because they are Muslims but rather they feel Muslim because of jihad' (Marranci 2006: 158). In other words, jihadists are individuals for whom jihad is the essential act of their identity so that they may *feel* their autobiographical self (Damasio 2003) as Islamic. Hence, in this specific case, I argue that the term 'jihadist' is appropriate.[4]

Understanding this phenomenon required, however, an approach that does not observe it in isolation, but instead views it as being part of a dynamic. As we have seen in Chapter 2, authors such as Huntington (1996) suggested that the liberal and democratic Western civilization and the supposedly oppressive and undeveloped Islamic civilization were culturally incompatible, an idea that the mass media and politicians would popularize as the War on Terror versus Jihad. It is my contention here that the dynamic has less to do with *culture* and geopolitical essentialism and more to do with human emotions. Fear is among the most prominent emotions a person can experience. Fear shall have a central role in our discussion at the end of this chapter. It is necessary, however, that I first clarify my position on emotions. Indeed, Ben-Ze'ev introduced the study of emotions with a certain pessimistic view: 'The nature, causes, and consequences of the emotions are among the least understood aspects of human experience' (2000: xiii). Yet, in the last ten years, psychology and neurology have provided new material which anthropologists can integrate in their understandings of emotions. I may positively say that, today, emotions are no longer mysterious.

Scholars have acknowledged that what we call *emotions* possess at least two different meanings: one pertaining to the physical body and the other to social and cultural domains. Inevitably the study of emotions has suffered from dualisms, with some scholars arguing that, despite the evident biological aspects, 'emotions have a social ontology ... a social-relational genesis' (Lyon 1998, quoted in Milton 2007: 63); therefore, emotions are predominately cultural and are mainly ideas, so that 'emotion as an idea is socially and culturally manufactured, as also is emotion as a reality. ... The idea is that emotion is private and internal; the reality is that it is intrinsically interpersonal and communicative or performative' (Parkinson 1995: 25). Within the humanities and, in particular, until recently within sociology and anthropology, scholars have suggested that emotions are culturally constructed (see, for instance, Geertz 1973; Heelas 2007; Lutz 2007).[5] For instance, Harré has 'censured' the idea that emotions may be part of physiological processes as no more than an 'ontological illusion' (1986: 6). Instead, he has argued that scholars must observe how words, such as 'anger', are used in specific cultural contexts. Harré, like a great majority of constructivists, has rejected any neuroscientific discoveries and has reduced the biological factors of emotions to secondary factors derived from our 'Pleistocene' past.

On the contrary, evolutionary psychologists and cognitive anthropologists have suggested that emotions are 'superordinate programs' which regulate our behaviour so that we can adapt to the specific problems that the environment poses to humans (Cosmides and Tooby 2000). Izard went even further and argued that emotions 'constitute the primary motivational system for human beings' (Izard 1977: 3). Compared to twenty or thirty years ago, neuroscientific research has added a significant contribution to the study of emotions. Although symbols and social interactions are relevant to the understanding of emotions (Milton and Svasek 2005: 35; Milton 2002), scholars such as Harré seem to forget the essential role of consciousness and the relationship of the biological reactions to the neurological processing. Indeed, as Milton has argued, the 'other' producing the emotional behaviour 'does not have to be a social or human other; it can be anything with which the individual organism engages, for emotion is part of that engagement' (2005: 35). This leads to the conclusion that through engagement with different environments 'people learn to love, hate, fear, or be disgusted by different things, so that their body reacts differently when things are encountered' (2005: 36).

As an anthropologist, I have found that neurologist Damasio's views on emotions provide that necessary balance to avoid both the ontologies that have affected their study. Damasio (2004) has observed a simple fact: the word 'emotion' in English (but also other languages) includes the meaning 'feeling'. Yet, he has identified two different processes and for clarity he has distinguished 'emotions' from 'feelings' (see also Kringelbach 2004). The word emotions, according to Damasio, identifies the biological changes in the individual body, such as an increased heart rate, sweating, high blood pressure and the like (who has not experienced the famous symptom of nervousness – butterflies in the stomach – before an exam?). Emotions are, therefore, internal reactions to external stimuli. Most of these reactions are automatic and you do not need to be conscious of them (and in the great majority of cases, you will not be). Yet, these physiological changes will not be enough for you to describe an emotion. Damasio identified another aspect, the 'feelings'. He has defined feelings as being mental representations of the body-state; they are the private experience of emotions, inaccessible to observation and consequently to other fellow humans. In other words, emotions pertain to the domain of the body, while feelings pertain to the domain of the mind.

Although these are rather simple concepts, Damasio's differentiation between emotions and feelings forces us to rethink the relationship between the two when the temporal element is added; and this can be counterintuitive. We have just said that feelings are the mental representations of the body-state. This means that first an individual experiences the physiological changes (i.e. emotion) and *then the mental representation of those changes*. In other words, you are not first sad and then cry, but rather you cry and then feel sad. While emotions do not become part of the mind, as they are strictly reactions to external stimuli, feelings become a significant part of the mind as the lasting memory of emotions. Happiness, joy, love, empathy and other more complex 'sentiments' are not (as common sense understands them) emotions but rather, in Damasio's terms, feelings: 'The chain that begins with the triggering of emotions and continues with the execution of emotion continues with the establishment of the substrates for feeling in the appropriate body-sensing brain regions' (Damasio 2004: 65).

If we, as I do, accept Damasio's theory of emotions, we can conclude that experience and environment have much more of an impact than could be expected from the constructivist view. It also means that you do not need particular social interactions to develop certain feelings through the emotions provoked by the external stimuli. As we shall see this in this chapter, this is very important to understanding the dynamic of jihadists as civilizers. Of course, it is worth remembering that emotions (so the physiological changes) and feelings (the derived mental processes) have a very deep impact on how memories are formed, the autobiographical self shaped and identity developed. While the autobiographical self is part of our neural plasticity and can be located in parts of the brain, identity is a machinery of our imagination which helps us to maintain a focused sense of the autobiographical self. When we add to this the fact that there is no such thing as emotion-free religiosity, 'it is not a question of *whether* emotions influence our religious thinking, but rather a matter of *which* emotions most strongly mobilise the subprograms that collectively constitute our perception and cognition' (Fuller 2006: 45, emphasis in the original), and we may start to appreciate the complexity involved in understanding the rhetoric of jihad.

Yet as we shall see, emotions and feelings by themselves cannot explain why some (and a minority) people become violent in thought and sometimes in action. We need to understand the processes that make some of them 'jihadists', as they now tend to call themselves. To do so, I will combine two theories: one is from the field of criminology and the other from psychology. Using general strain theory and the standard model of cognitive dissonance, I shall explain the processes through which a small number of Muslims become radicalized, with some of them becoming violent civilizers, instead of simply stopping at the rhetoric of civilization. Before doing so, however, I wish to introduce a specific case study involving 'Irhabi007', Terrorist 007, the online nickname of a young Moroccan who I had the occasion to know during my research. During our time together, I was able to study the dynamics that made him one of the most elusive but also wanted 'internet jihadis' who, according to the prosecution in the UK, had also moved towards a more active jihadist role in real life.

The case of Irhabi 007

What pushes a young Muslim to be involved in violent jihad against the 'West' while living and benefiting from the freedoms and consumerism of the same place s/he wants to attack? What dynamic can transform a law-abiding shy teen from a middle-class migrant family into a 'cyber jihadi' who hopes for martyrdom in Iraq?

In late 2007, during my research on Muslims in prison (Marranci 2009), I was contacted by the young Moroccan's lawyers. They wanted me to be an expert witness for their client who was arrested and accused of possessing propaganda (in the form of e-books, videos, audio recordings and online chat conversations) linked to al-Qaida in Iraq and possessing videos glorifying 9/11 and distributing the material online, as well as committing other serious offences, such as preparing others for suicide actions or martyrdom in Iraq and organizing attacks in Europe. The young man was none other than the elusive 'Irhabi007', Terrorist 007, an 'internet jihadi' and a member, according to the prosecution, of al-Qaida in northern Europe, and for which he had even designed the logo. His name: Younes Tsouli.

Arrested during a special police operation in 2005, his sad, battered face became iconic of the 'bedroom mujahedin' who plan their jihad against the West directly from the West's heartlands. The police had no idea, at the time, that the young man they had arrested in what they considered a low-profile operation was in reality what the mass media described as 'The world's most wanted cyber-jihadist'.[6] Younes was charged under the UK's Terrorism Act 2000 for 'conspiracy to murder, conspiracy to cause an explosion, conspiracy to obtain money by deception, fundraising and possession of articles for terrorist purposes'.[7]

For a few years Irhabi 007 had been a pioneer in the mediatization of al-Qaida's jihad. Many would go on to learn from his lessons and mistakes. As early as 2004, he joined and became administrator of two of the most popular password-protected al-Qaida forums, Muntada al-Ansar al-Islami (Islam Supporters Forum) and al-Ekhlas (Sincerity). This was the time when Abu Musab al-Zarqawi in Iraq was spreading videos of his organization's violent and bloody actions as well as propaganda messages to convince young Muslims to join the war in Iraq and to bring the violence to the doorstep of the West. As we know, such propaganda was very successful, as the 7/7 suicide bombing attack in 2005 demonstrated. Irhabi 007 became central to facilitating the spread of messages put out by Abu Maysara al-Iraqi, the spokesperson for al-Qaida in Iraq (what today has become ISIS). Messages such as 'a group of proud and brave men are ready to strike the economic interests of the countries of blasphemy and atheism, that came to raise the banner of the Cross in the country of the Muslims' were praised by Irhabi 007. He became a central figure facilitating the takeover of vulnerable internet servers to obtain free, unlimited space for videos and material provided by al-Qaida. As we shall see, he loved to be at the centre of attention and believed himself to be an active and real mujahid, which was, surely, how other members saw him. Indeed, one message in the Ansar forum was totally devoted to him (August 2004):

To Our Brother Irhabi 007. Our brother Irhabi 007, you have shown very good efforts in serving this message board, as I can see, and in serving jihad for the sake of God. By God, we do not like to hear what hurts you, so we ask God to keep you in his care. You are one of the top people who care about serving your brothers. May God add all of that on the side of your good work, and may you go careful and successful. We say carry on with God's blessing. Carry on, may God protect you. Carry on serving jihad and its supporters. And I ask the mighty, gracious and merciful God to keep for us everyone who wants to support his faith. Amen.

Yet, who was Younes beyond the Irhabi 007 persona? I can answer probably better than many others, since not only did I have full access to his hard disks and files but also was allowed insight into his personal life first when I had the opportunity to meet him in person at HM Prison Belmarsh three times before he pleaded guilty to all the charges and, afterwards, through written correspondence from his cell. Furthermore, and importantly, I had an occasion to interview his father. This allowed me to understand the process that turned a very young and shy Younes into the infamous Irhabi 007.

I met Younes when he was twenty-three. His father, who worked for the Moroccan Embassy in London, told me that his son joined him and his wife in the UK in 2001 and was granted indefinite leave to remain in the UK on the 24th of August 2005. He loved technology and studied IT at Westminster College of Computing. Younes was just an ordinary, young, and rather shy, man. His father reported that he had friends among non-Muslims and he was not restricted in whom he met. Younes seemed, however, more at ease in his room with his computer, and as his father said, 'He spent lots of time in chatrooms and in his room working on that thing, of which I did not understand very much.' Younes was very confident while engaging others in the virtual world of the internet, and he tended to trust everybody in that virtual space while demonstrating a lack of trust in people in real life. He tended to reject attempts to meet face to face, preferring the virtual world as an alternative social space.

Younes was fluent in French, Arabic and English and, indeed, he visited chatrooms and conducted search engine enquiries in those languages. His father pointed out, during the interview, that his son never appeared to show a particular interest in religion, and that while he prayed the five daily prayers, Younes seemed only to show interest in Ramadan and neglected many other aspects of Islam. His father said, 'We are a religious family, but moderate. I mean, we're normal people who respect God but that's it. Younes never showed particular interest in religion.'

Indeed, Younes seemed to be very much a youth of his age, interested in music and even girls. Although he was shy, it is clear from the analysis of his hard disks that pornography was among his interests. This is relevant because this interest did not cease during the period of his Irhabi 007 activities. In other words, Younes did not show a particular degree of respect for Islamic requirements. He was not a fervent believer. Yet, Younes had increasingly monitored Islamic forums and chatrooms at least since 2002–3. He classified files, took notes and recorded conversations and connections as much as possible. More than the situations in Afghanistan, Chechnya or Palestine, which were rarely mentioned in his communications, it was the US-led invasion of Iraq that appeared to stir something within him. This was confirmed by his father, who explained,

He became more and more interested in the War in Iraq. It seemed like an obsession. He started to challenge my ideas. He told me that I was reading the wrong news in the newspapers and that he had access to the real situation. I did not understand what he wanted to say at the time. I felt challenged and very upset about that. He became involved in anti-war movements, and I was not happy about that. We had very bad arguments. He wanted to take part in anti-war marches. I stopped him from it; I work for the Moroccan government and in the Moroccan Embassy. How can the son of an officer protest against the host government? Also, why? He had received great advantages from being here in the UK. I stopped him from discussing these things and from taking part in any activity related to the conflict.

Probably, this father-son conflict and the attitude of Younes' father towards the 'No War movement' prevented Younes from expressing his discontent towards the UK government's actions and policies. Younes' feelings about the unjust conflict and suffering of Muslims in Iraq and the emotions and feelings he could not express publicly may have been the main trigger to transform him into Irhabi 007. From chat conversations and material he collected, it is clear that he was very much affected by the plight of women and children in Iraq, which worsened starting from the embargo imposed by the United States. He had a fascination for military activities and appeared to fantasize about 'actions', adventure and heroism. Yet, of the radical forum members, Irhabi 007 employed less religious rhetoric, using few of the basic expressions that Muslims often exchange, such as religious greetings and various Arabic phrases. Irhabi 007 surely had a sense of humour, showed great self-esteem, considered himself an expert in the field of hacking and was very generous with his time to help others, but only in that virtual social space that appeared to be at the same time his life and grave.

Younes in his Irhabi 007 persona dreamt about adventure on the battlefield, yet he was stuck at his desk watching the screen of his laptop. He made contacts through the internet and hoped to use them one day for his never-to-come mujahideen experience, in which he would be a freedom fighter who rescued oppressed Muslim women and children. Younes enjoyed a Western lifestyle and security, including free and unrestricted access to pornography which British laws allowed, and he was definitely 'Westernized'. The disillusionment with British politics was, perhaps, particularly strong precisely because of this Westernization experience, which, as we shall discuss below, produced in him a cognitive dissonance. The war in Iraq, which started in March 2003, had an extraordinary impact on him and some other young Muslims. The disastrous invasion and brutal occupation of Iraq, the graphic images available through the Arab mass media, as well as the shocking stories to emerge from Abu Ghraib prison not only increased the alienation of many of these young people but also induced what I can define as a morbid attraction to ideas of sacrifice and heroic death.

Indeed, these young Muslims shared the advantages of Western societies as well as its illnesses. The case of Abu Ghraib in 2004, in particular, highlighted to many a perceived lack of real values and the hypocrisy of Western self-celebration. In the majority of cases, this disaffection was expressed through a rhetoric that exalted the heroic and mythical actions of the 'lions of the two rivers', 'the soldiers of Allah', the martyrs and the 'avengers of God'. Black flags, logos featuring Qur'anic verses and Kalashnikovs, and images of armies of white and black horses were saved as desktop backgrounds, screen savers and on mobile phones. Rambo turned into Al-Zarqawi, the leader of Al-Qaida in Iraq, who was perceived as someone who was a mixture of Herod and Robin Hood. Young men who were very vulnerable, impressionable and without much in the way of resources could at least show off their masculinity and bravado by playing jihad. Younes was one of them, and he became a master in his own virtual jihad by becoming Irhabi 007. After his arrest, he decided, to the great surprise of his defence team, to plead guilty to all charges despite it being clear that some of them could have been easily challenged in court. He was sentenced to serve twelve years in prison, which was soon increased to sixteen years after an appeal by the prosecution. This sentence, at the time, was the highest penalty imposed on a young person who had not committed a violent criminal act. During the years prior to his incarceration, Younes had to face the condemnation of his own father, as well as the impossibility of taking part in demonstrations or participating in any other form of democratic protest. Such limitations, as we shall see while discussing the general strain theories, may have contributed to the path the young Younes took.

Younes, like many other young Muslims who follow the path of jihad, felt he was part of a divine plan and accepted his destiny in prison – this was probably preferable to his mother, but he would have preferred the 'blessed grave' and the reward of paradise that the mujahideen expect over the cold, grey walls of a prison cell.

Drones, emotional Islam and a-Justice

He asked me: what is the ruling on blowing up the neighbourhood where an army general responsible for killing Muslim civilians' lives? I said this is wrong and not permissible as this causes innocent people to die, including women and children. He said OK, but what is the ruling on US drones attacking Muslim civilians in Yemen and Afghanistan, also killing women and children? I said: this is also wrong and a criminal act and must not be allowed by any Muslim or non-Muslim country. He said: then why are you stopping us and not stopping them? (Facebook comment in a closed Islamic group)

Imams[8] in both the United Kingdom and Australia have reported to me that they have received very similar questions. Islamic forums, Facebook pages and groups also tend to have a high number of comments and posts that reflect very similar questions to the above. It is not difficult to read in such questions both a certain bravado and a provocative attitude instead of real threats of imminent violence. Muslims living in Western countries, in particular the youth, feel that there is not only a deep injustice affecting Muslim communities around the world, but also that there is a high degree of hypocrisy originating from what they have identified as the West (see Chapter 4 in this book). The drones, the Hellfire missiles and the 'collateral damage', which often involves women and children, become the iconic symbols of such asymmetric values. Muslims must condemn each and every terrorist attack wherever it may happen and for any reason, but what about their own victims; what about Muslims? This is the question that many ask themselves and each other. This question comes with a pointed finger aimed at 'Western' societies.

> The West and the nature of its crusade hasn't changed much. In fact much more violence is being perpetrated with the precision and inhuman firepower of drones, missiles, bombs that has turned whole countries like Iraq and Afghanistan into graveyards. Only the Khilafah system, a system that comes from Allah, the maker of man, can liberate mankind from destroying itself. The Justice and Shade of Allah's Throne – this is the true Peace and Mercy Allah has promised to those who seek honour from nowhere but Islam. (Post in a closed Facebook Islamic group)

The rhetoric of the civilizer is central to the understanding of emotions and feelings (understood in Damasio's terms) that some Muslims experience when considering such world issues. Also central is the concept of *ummah*. It is evident that many Muslims living in the West do not feel part of it despite asserting their right, for instance, to be Australian, French, Italian or British. The 'West', in other words, is an oppositional category to 'the *ummah*'.

> We as Muslims have our beliefs that define us while they don't! Their justice and democracy is a big lie that, unfortunately, some Muslims are endorsing and believing in! This so called civilised world that considers slaughtering animals barbaric looks the other way when civilians are slaughtered by US drones. Any Muslim who doesn't speak against such attacks is a sinner. (Comment on a post in a closed Facebook Islamic group)

Terms such as 'West' and 'ummah' have lost their original meaning and acquired a civilizational one, as we have discussed in previous parts of this book. This is a very important process that we need to analyse to fully appreciate the complexity of the dynamics we are experiencing today. The 'West' and its governments are *kufr*, while the Islamic system, expressed often through the word sharia, is the civilized way. It is no surprise that some young Muslims see the mujahideen as the last bastion of resistance for the 'Muslim way of life', as illustrated in the following comment.

> Kufaar have latest weapons far better than weapons used by mujahideen. …uThey have planes, drones, missiles, latest communication systems, world media, submarines, ships everything that u can imagine. … Still the lions of Allah are fighting the world's greatest armies with handheld weapons i.e. with AK47s, RPG3s, mortars, BM missiles, pistols, light machine guns etc. … Still alhamdulillah we are on the winning side by the grace of Allah. … Yes Sahaba r.a. were best of All … but our mujahid brothers are trying their best too by the grace of Allah. … If Muslims had the help of angels in the battle of Badar, why can't Allah send angels again????? We should appreciate our mujahid brothers who are fighting kufaar alhamdulillah. (Comment on a post in a closed Facebook Islamic group)

But which mujahideen? Which sharia? The interesting fact is that these young Muslims living in Western nations lack the knowledge of those living in the affected Middle East regions. All groups, from al-Qaida to the more recent ISIS, appear to the disoriented, young Muslims to be expressions of one single entity, an entity providing the resistance of the *ummah* against the barbaric West, a resistance perceived as a fight to maintain the Islamic civilization, to bring the 'true' way of life to humanity.

> They consider the way of living that was recommended by the creator as barbaric, but what they suggest is not only barbaric but animalistic. Allah's recommendation will always be the best for all times. Western democracy my foot! (Comment on a post in a closed Facebook Islamic group)

The lack of awareness that these young Muslims have of the differing stances of Islamic resistance groups, or even the lack of interest in learning about the various factions and the differing ideologies they express, is per se a very clear symptom of what I call 'emotional Islam'.

The term emotional Islam identifies a process by which Islam is not experienced as a religion dependent upon a particular theology and theological discourse that are historical in origin and linked to traditions, but rather as independent values, or in other words, an 'ethos' (see Chapter 2 in this book), which is affected by context and environment that provoke emotions that are experienced as feelings. Emotional Islam essentializes some aspects of Islam, such as the concept of justice. Although it is an essential element of Islam, justice is never a theologically isolated and independent variable. Even the justice of Allah is not fully and solely retributive, but instead nearly mysterious as expressed often in the Qur'an and hadiths (Barazangi, Zaman and Afzal 1996). Yet in emotional Islam, 'justice' becomes an essence that goes beyond the theological meaning; it becomes a civilizer's tool, a powerful element in defining who is human and what matters to the ethos of being human.

The concept of 'justice' is not just an abstract philosophical idea, but rather, as some scholars have argued (Hauser 2006), it derives from a cognitive process, the so-called moral faculty. There are also several studies that show the deep connection between emotions, feelings (often referred to in these studies as 'affects') and the perception of justice (Cropanzano, Stein and Nadisic 2010; Weiss, Suckow and Cropanzano 1999). Research has shown that not just humans (Buunk and Schaufeli 1999) but also primates (Brosnan 2006; de Waal 1996) have an evolutionary based aversion to unfair treatment.

Justice (or the lack of it) provokes emotions, feelings and, of course, the strong actions and reactions that can follow. You need only to remember an episode in which you suffered injustice (or so you perceived) to have an emotional reaction; your blood pressure may raise, you may start to feel your heart rate increase, and perhaps you may even feel a strange sensation in your stomach. These are 'emotions', yet these emotions will be translated into feelings, such as the feeling of being upset, angry, disappointed and so forth. Tomaka et al. have suggested that 'one could argue that the justice paradigm can be understood as a special instance of the more general appraisal models of emotions and that the typical justice situation can be seen as an affective event' (1994: 787).

As Cropanzano, Stein and Nadisic (2010) have demonstrated, the idea that emotional processes affect how justice is perceived and conceptualized is not novel. Indeed, renowned scholars such as Solomon have observed,

> Emotions are essential to our sense of justice, and this includes such negative emotions as vengeance as well as such positive emotions as sympathy and compassion. ... Understanding the emotions that go into our sense of justice, learning how these are cultivated and giving them new respect, rather than further developing the already voluminous arguments for and against this or that intellectual construction of justice, seems to be essential. (Solomon 1989: 372)

Yet, there is another relevant concept that we must consider to understand the processes through which civilizers are reacting to the present wars of terror and also taking part: *dignity*.

Boltanski and Chiapello (2005: 491) have noticed that 'forms of indignation may be regarded as emotional expressions of a meta-ethical anchorage, and concern infringements that are believed, at least implicitly, to affect people's possibilities of realising their humanity'. Solomon goes further and shows how 'emotions ascribe responsibility, which is utterly essential to our sense of justice. We do not first ascribe responsibility and then respond emotionally. The emotion itself ascribes responsibility; it immediately recognises (or simply presumes) that a harm or hurt has a cause. ... Injustice, in other words, is not just getting the short end; it also requires that someone be to blame' (Solomon 1990: 255). In the world views of civilizers, both 'dignity' and 'somebody to blame' is essential to reinforcing the in-group unity and sense of identity.

On the one hand, for those who see themselves as expressions of a 'Judeo-Christian' identity and civilizational mission, Muslims not only lack dignity but are also a threat to the dignity of the 'West'. They, of course, see the 'barbaric' customs of Muslims, such as the sharia, as the ultimate form of injustice and as a direct assault on the dignity of Western understandings of human rights and secularism. We need to bear in mind that these perceptions are not just abstract intellectual observations and arguments; rather, they have deep emotional effects on the civilizer and his or her views of the world.

On the other hand, in the case of those civilizers who see themselves as the ultimate defenders of Islam, it is the West, with its secularized Judaeo-Christian identity and values, which lacks not only dignity, but also the concept of justice. Indeed, according to them, justice can be only with a capital J, the Justice of God: eternal, immutable and unquestionable. This viewpoint, as my research has shown, makes the Muslim civilizer understand the West not as a place that is unjust, but as a place of a-justice, where justice simply doesn't exist. The Islam that derives from these feelings is characterized by a strong reaction to the West, which is no longer perceived as a geographical expression, location or even culture, but rather as a symbol of kufr: a-just, morally indigent and, of course, threatening to the Truth and only civilized 'way of life'.

Allah swt [subhana wa ta'ala i.e. Glorified and Exalted is He] tells us in Surah Al-Baqarah that that non-Muslims will never be happy with us until we follow their way. In our current times it's similar to how we are expected to collapse all our traditions, culture, beliefs, practices, attitudes & behaviour to integrate and assimilate into the mainstream way of being. So, ideally, we should not expect or anticipate that they would accept us, so trying to appease them will only lead us to lose our own sense of self. We can still hold onto our sense of 'self' (individual and community) whilst participating in the environment in which we live, however, we just need to be strong enough not to compromise so much and to work through reclaiming our own traditions so that they are not inadvertently erased by our own doings. (Public Facebook comment from an Australian Muslim woman)

The above statement, which is very representative of even those considered 'moderate' Muslims, as its author indeed is, provides a good example of the sense of incompatibility that 'civilizers' perceive towards difference. Here, there is no longer a problem of tolerance or acceptance, but rather there is a problem of opposed ethos. Muslim civilizers can only participate 'in the environment', instead of within the communities or society in which they live and this participation is based on 'howevers'. The decontextualized quotation from the Qur'an is used to emphasize the difference in ethos between those who hold the key to being considered 'real' humans and those who are anti-humans because of their lack of certain values – the 'traditions, culture, beliefs, practices, attitudes & behaviour' referred to above. In this statement, the perception of 'otherness' is such that no commonality can be found and there can instead only be a winner and a loser in a battle of ethos, where 'trying to appease them will only lead us to lose our own sense of self'. The machinery of imagination called 'identity' that allows a unified sense of self is here expressed through an axiom: feeling Muslim is essentially feeling different from non-Muslims and thus, being, truly human.

Some respondents during my years of research have expressed such passive resistance to maintain 'traditions, culture, beliefs, practices, attitudes & behaviour' as jihad (Marranci 2006). In a majority of cases, this jihad is psychological, performative and based on avoidance rather than violence. Yet, some pass from the resistance to violence, which can be expressed nonviolently or degenerate into violent acts, such as, in extreme cases, terrorism. 'Jihadis' are those who, as we have seen, shift from their rejection of what they perceive as a non-Islamic ethos to actively punishing such a lack of ethos, and the accompanying a-justice. Instead of being sudden, often the shift is made gradually through a process where the civilizer passes from the rhetoric of civilization to the act of civilization, which may include a terrorist act, intended to teach a lesson and indeed, ultimately, civilize.

Some young Muslims today may feel disoriented because of messages like the above that they hear within their own communities. Born and raised in the West, they may be made to feel guilty for being part of it by previous generations and, at the same time, they are inevitably also accused of not being integrated within the mainstream society. An young Australian Muslim, during a personal chat conversation, noticed,

It's like so bad for the Muslim youth in that if they turn towards the western way, they are targeted for raping whores, or dealing drugs, but if they are good muslims who want to be seeing Australia do the right thing they are damned as well.

Many studies[9] acknowledge the pressure that mainstream Western societies have applied on young Muslims. What is lacking, instead, is a research investigation into the pressure that these third- and fourth-generation Muslims suffer from within their own Muslim communities. Indeed, a certain scholarly approach to these issues tends to repeat postcolonial views where the 'West' is the culprit and the minority the victim of endless colonization. These views, although surely partially true, have missed the existing dynamics and absolved one part of the equation. Young Muslims are often scrutinized by family and their religious community, expected to uphold traditions, culture, beliefs, practices, attitudes and behaviour seen as epitome of being 'Muslim'. They are also expected to 'hold onto' their 'sense of "self" (individual and community)', which should be, of course, Islamic, a conception of which is, in turn, in many instances ontologically incompatible with what the community perceives as the 'West' (an understanding evident in the remark that was reproduced above – 'non-Muslims will never be happy with us until [Muslims] follow their way').

Should it then be a surprise that an increasing number of young Muslims born and raised in Australia or in other Western countries, or even those who have converted to Islam, support extremist groups such as ISIS or dream – and in a few cases enact the dream – about travelling to be part of the mujahideen who strive to build the perfect home where no contradiction may be found, where justice with the capital 'J' may be enforced and where you can be only one thing, a real human, a Muslim?

Strains, cognitive dissonance and emotional Islam

We have seen that there are clear differences between those who are part of resistance movements resisting the invasion of a country, such as Afghanistan and Iraq, and those who see themselves as 'jihadis' or even 'terrorists'. The main distinction is the impact of what I have called 'emotional Islam' as part of their civilizing visions. Those acquainted with criminology studies may not be surprised to read that those who commit acts of violence or those who invite others to do so in the name of (emotional) Islam are normally aged between eighteen and twenty-eight years old or, at any length, those who may be categorized as 'youth'. Indeed, studies have shown that this is the age bracket in which criminal acts are more common due to the fact that young people are more prone to take risks and act upon their ideas and perceptions (Sweeten, Piquero and Steinberg 2013; Farrington 1986). I mention 'crime' here, since there is a certain affinity between 'jihadi' actions and what may be defined as 'criminality', as we have seen in the case of Irhabi 007. Some scholars have suggested that crime theories may provide an understanding of what pushes some individuals to engage in terrorist acts (see, for instance, Rosenfeld 2002; LaFree and Dugan 2004; Rausch and LaFree 2007) and they have done so by employing strain-based explanations of terrorism, where grievance has a central role, with some scholars such as Rosenfeld (2004: 23) noticing that 'without a grievance, there would be no terrorism'. The idea of strain as a cause of crime was for the first time developed by Merton as part of his anomie study (1938).

Robert Merton has provided a discussion and theory of social structure and anomie which has become very popular within criminology (Featherstone and Deflem 2003). Despite the fact that the theory was published in 1938, the impact of it has reached current research, since Merton's framework has provided the starting point for new theoretical approaches and developments (for a list, see Adler and Laufer 1995; Passas and Agnew 1997). Merton, according to Featherstone and Deflem (2003), had in reality developed two distinct frameworks which tend to become confused, the first of which is a theory of anomie that partially derives from Durkheim's work (Marks 1974).

Merton's anomie is the product of a process of deinstitutionalization of norms that derives from a disjunction between a strong focus on cultural norms and institutional means (Merton 1938: 673; 1968: 189), or 'a specific imbalance where cultural goals are overemphasised at the expense of institutionalised means' (Orrù 1987: 122). Merton acknowledged that individuals may adjust in different ways to anomic conditions. The most easy to observe is the 'conformity', the acceptance of the social structure pressure. Yet, some individuals will not conform and react to the social structure pressure through what he has called 'retreatism', or rejecting the goals and means of society; 'rebellion', which includes not just rejection of the values but also an attempt to substitute them; 'ritualism' in which goals are unreachable but despite that the norms are still respected; and 'innovation', where goals are accepted but there is a rejection of the means to reach them.

The second framework that Merton developed is strain theory. He suggested that individuals who are prevented from attaining culturally prescribed goals through institutionalized means may instead resort to illegitimate means (Merton 1938: 679; 1968: 211). In a famous remark, Merton pointed out that 'social structure strains the cultural values, making action in accord with them readily possible for those occupying certain statuses within the society and difficult or impossible for others' (1968: 216–17). For him, however, it was 'wealth goals' which individuals, if restrained, may try to achieve through illegal means due to the cultural value that American society adduces to economic success. Of course, from this viewpoint, the disadvantaged classes are more prone to crime than others. Many scholars have criticized Merton's strain theory exactly for not considering other aspects, and empirical research seemed to challenge what however appeared to be a very logical and strong theoretical framework (Hindelang, Hirschi and Weis 1982; Thornberry and Farnworth 1982; Krohn et al. 1980; Johnson 1979) Merton acknowledged some of the criticism and wrote some papers (Merton 1995; 1997a, b) aimed at addressing the ambiguities between the theories of anomie and strain as well as their overly economic focus.

Merton's anomie and, in particular, strain theory seem to fit particularly well when we try to explain why some young people decide to embark on a 'jihadi' path. They clearly face social structural pressures and they are prevented from achieving their goals through acceptable social means. While the majority of Muslims conform to the social structure and many engage in 'retreatism', a certain number will take the 'rebellion' path. Yet, I have suggested in this chapter that emotions and feelings may be essential to the process that brings some 'civilizers' to perceive 'rebellion' as the only acceptable means of expressing their worldview. Agnew's very influential research and development of general strain theory (1985, 1989, 1992, 2001, 2006) may help us consider the role of emotions and feelings in the process. Indeed, Agnew has criticized, among others, the narrow focus and theorization of Merton's strain theory (Agnew 1985, 1989). Instead of stopping at criticism, however, he redeveloped the concept (1992, 2006). In his revision, Agnew identified other essential elements as part of the strain process, such as a lack of positive stimuli and an existence of negative emotions, such as anger and depression (Agnew 2001); as Broidy (2001: 10) has observed,

> According to general strain theory, strain triggers negative emotions, which in turn necessitate coping. If legitimate coping strategies are either ineffective or unavailable, an individual is likely to adopt illegitimate coping strategies. General strain theory identifies three types of strain – the failure to achieve positively valued goals, the removal of positively valued stimuli, and the presentation of negative stimuli.

It is very relevant to our study how Agnew has defined 'strain' compared to the rather vague definition of Merton. Agnew has observed that strains are 'relationships in which others are not treating the individual as he or she would like to be treated' (1992: 48); the solution for some individuals will be to prevent, reacquire or try to manage the lost positive stimuli or try to stop the negative stimuli.

Agnew, however, has acknowledged that not all individuals exposed to negative stimuli or loss of positive stimuli express themselves with deviant behaviours. He suggested that four characteristics of strain are the most common to induce such deviancy from social structural norms: 'The characteristics of those types of strain most likely to lead to crime are described. Briefly, such strains (1) are seen as unjust, (2) are seen as high in magnitude, (3) are associated with low social control, and (4) create some pressure or incentive to engage in crime' (2001: 320). Several empirical studies have provided evidence to support general strain theory and the fact that there is a strong positive relationship between strain and deviance (Aseltine, Gore and Gordon 2000; Bao, Haas and Pi 2004; Baron 2004; Broid 2001; Jang and Johnson 2003; Mazerolle and Maah 2000; Mazerolle and Piquero 1997; Moon and Morash, 2004; Piquero and Sealock 2000) as well as the role of emotions in strain (what Damasio has called 'feelings'), as for instance Ganem (2010) has noticed.

Agnew (2010), noticing that strain approaches to terrorism suffer from very much the same weaknesses seen in Merton's analysis (Agnew 2010: 132–5), has instead suggested that his general strain theory provides a much more complex framework to understand terrorist actions; thus, he has argued that terrorism is more likely

> when people experience 'collective strains' that are: (a) high in magnitude, with civilians affected; (b) unjust; and (c) inflicted by significantly more powerful others, including 'complicit' civilians, with whom members of the strained collectivity have weak ties. These collective strains increase the likelihood of terrorism because they increase negative emotions, reduce social control, reduce the ability to cope through legal and military channels, foster the social learning of terrorism, and contribute to a collective orientation and response.

The problem is that Agnew, like many other criminologists, has only focused on 'terrorism' and has studied mainly movements instead of individuals. It is my contention that when we combine Damasio's understanding of emotions, feelings and identity (the aspects concerning the ideology of justice and the perception of ethos in what I have defined as emotional Islam), we can finally have a very good framework to understand how individual civilizers may pass from the rhetoric of jihad to violent actions.

Yet, to make sense of the process, there is a final piece of the mosaic that it is needed. Indeed, if general strain theory explains how emotions and the feeling of injustice may help some descend into deviance, the question remains why some people do not take such a path despite being in a similar environment as well as perhaps being themselves civilizers in terms of their worldviews. The answer can be found when we combine Agnew's theory with a less popular but surely well-demonstrated and validated theory: Stone and Cooper's (2001) 'self-standards model of cognitive dissonance'. Some Muslims, particularly in the West as we have seen from some of the forum discussions, are experiencing uncomfortable tensions due to their experience of contrary values, which is what, in other words, we could call inconsistent cognitions. Festinger suggested that cognition is 'the things a person knows about himself, about his behaviour, and about his surroundings' (1957: 9), and from that observation he progressed to develop what is known as his 'theory of cognitive dissonance'. He observed: 'The holding of two or more inconsistent cognitions arouses the state of cognitive dissonance, which is experienced as uncomfortable tension. This tension has drive-like properties and must be reduced' (Festinger 1957, quoted in Cooper 2007: 7). Festinger observed that people can reduce dissonance in three main ways: '1. By changing one or more of the elements involved in dissonant relations. 2. By adding new cognitive elements that are consonant with already existing cognition. 3. By decreasing the importance of the elements involved in the dissonant relations' (1957: 264). In other words, the easiest way to reduce such a tension is to change, rather abruptly, ideas, opinions and behaviours. As Graham and Weiner (1996: 20) has so correctly noticed, 'If one changes his opinion about the issue at hand, the behaviour is no longer dissonant with the opinion, and dissonance is reduced. Also, if one changes his behaviour and the behaviour now matches the opinion, dissonance is reduced.'

Recently, Stone and Cooper (2001) have expanded and refined Festinger's theory and developed the self standard model of cognitive dissonance. They have suggested that the trigger to the arousal of cognitive dissonance is a person's consideration of the outcomes of behaviour. They observed, by starting from Higgins's self-discrepancy theory (Higgins 1989), that people use two main standards of judgement to assess the consequences of their behaviour. On the one hand, the 'normative' standard of judgement is based on what the majority of people in a group or culture may consider immoral, negative or in any other way wrong. On the other, the personal self-standard is based on one's own values, which may or may not be similar to the normative ones. Stone and Cooper have defined idiographic dissonance as being the arousal derived from the comparison between behavioural outcomes and personal standards. By contrast, they have defined nomothetic dissonance as being the arousal derived from judgements based on normative standards.

Many psychological studies and experiments have demonstrated the validity of the above model (see Cooper 2007). Recently, a neuroscientific study (Van Veen et al. 2009) has identified the dorsal anterior cingulate cortex and anterior insula as areas engaged during cognitive dissonance and that the activation of such areas correctly predicted participants' subsequent attitude change. It is interesting to notice how Damasio (Damasio 2004: 105) has pointed to the insula as one of the somatosensory regions that is most involved in the feeling process. Several experiments (Stone and Cooper 2001) in cognitive dissonance have confirmed that people will try to reduce the sense of psychological discomfort that dissonance causes, and the most efficient way to achieve this is to justify their behaviour or turn the negative experience of their action into a positive one. For civilizers, their often aggressive views, even when they do not become violent actions, are reinterpreted as a 'positive' part of their lives since such views (or actions) become spiritual salvation, or rather the salvation of 'civilization'.

Conclusion

What brings a young person to leave the security of his or her home in Sydney, Australia, and join a violent conflict in distant places such as Syria or Iraq under the banner of ISIS or other Islamic terrorist groups? What pushes a teenager, just eighteen years old, who has lived all his life in western Sydney, to commit a suicide attack in a Shia mosque in Iraq, killing three and injuring more than ninety?[10] In this chapter, we have explored, from a cognitive as well as a neuroanthropological approach, the deeper reasons behind those having civilizational world views reaching a point where they see violence as the only legitimate solution. Indeed, it is my contention that, although sociopolitical aspects have a deep relevance in decisions to join jihadi groups, the ultimate explanation of why so few Muslims actually join them may be found in the processes I have highlighted above. This means that although civilizational world views and ethos are not uncommon among Muslims both in the West and in Muslim countries, the actual 'Muslim civilizers' who are prepared to use violence and terrorism are extremely few.

Hence, it is no surprise that we can find a very high number of, for instance, Twitter and Facebook statements and comments that clearly employ civilizational rhetoric, which is often linked, as we have seen, to requests for 'justice' and 'dignity'. Yet, this obviously does not translate into the same number of individuals taking the dangerous path of full radicalization. In the case of Younes, the process that brought him to become Irhabi 007 may be explained through the combination of both general strain theory and the self standard model of cognitive dissonance. We need also to understand that people like Younes and those who, like him, become active jihadis are not reacting only to their own feelings and conditions, but rather are also often reacting to other civilizers and civilizational worldviews which are opposed to Islam and Muslims (although, as we have seen in this book, they are deeply similar in the processes that produce them). In my book *Jihad Beyond Islam* (2006), I have identified a process that, borrowing from Bhabha (1994), I have called 'the circle of panic'.

Bhabha explained how 'the indeterminate circulation of meaning as rumour or conspiracy' can have 'perverse, physical affects of panic' (1994: 200). We have discussed elsewhere in this book conspiracy theories which civilizers tend to spread, trust and support; we have also analysed the effects of stereotyping and demonizing the Other. What we see are not isolated, parallel factors, but rather what Bateson, while studying the Iatmul tribe (1936), identified as schismogenesis. Schismogenesis, observed Bateson, is 'characterized by interchanges of behaviour such as that the more A exhibited a given behaviour, the more B was likely to exhibit the same behaviour' (2002: 98). In other words, we may observe an escalation between two sides that is parallel and where both sides reinforce each other in a kind of race. This symmetrical escalation is what he called schismogenesis. Civilizers are indeed affected by schismogenesis, and this, in turn, affects their identities and, in some cases, modifies their understanding of Islam (i.e. produces emotional Islam) or the West as ethos (i.e. produces the idea of a moral superiority of the West). Part of the schismogenesis is, as we shall discuss in the conclusion, the struggle for civilizers to impose their understanding of what makes humans human and of who may be considered human. The competition is in the attempt to dehumanize the Other, and when this happens, the passage from a rhetoric of terror to an act of terror is easy. While some call for more jihad against the terrorist, a-just West, others invoke drones, new laws that curtail civil rights, torture and bombing of countries and communities. There is not a 'War on terror', but rather there are wars of terror.

Notes

1 Latika Bourke 'Number of Australians fighting with militants in Iraq and Syria "extraordinary", Julie Bishop says' ABC News Thu 19 June 2014, http://www.abc.net.au/news/2014-06-19/150-australians-fighting-with-extremists-in-iraq-and-syria/5535018 (accessed 20 June 2014).

2 Adam Withnall 'Iraq crisis: Isis 'has recruited at least 1,500 Britons' to fight abroad, warns Birmingham MP' The Independent Friday 27 June 2014, http://www.independent.co.uk/news/uk/home-news/iraq-crisis-isis-has-recruited-at-least-1500-britons-to-fight-abroad-warns-birmingham-mp-9556790.html (accessed 27 June 2014).

3 Lisa Cox 'Passports of Australian jihadists cancelled, says Julie Bishop' The Sydney Morning Herald, 22 June 2014, http://www.smh.com.au/federal-politics/political-news/passports-of-australian-jihadists-cancelled-says-julie bishop-20140622-3aly1.html#ixzz35owao4N9 (accessed 23 June 2014).

4 For a discussion of how I have understood Muslim identity as part of human identity, please refer to Marranci (2008), Ch. 6.

5 Among many other scholars privileging such constructivist approaches to emotions, it is worth mentioning Rosaldo (1984), Wentworth and Yardley (1994), Lupton (1998).

6 Corera (2008).

7 Katz and Kern (2006).

8 'Imam' refers to a person who leads the Muslim prayer and guides a particular Muslim community.

9 See Abbas (2007), Leiken (2005), Lewis (2007), Ozyurt (2013), Pauly (2013), Nagra and Peng (2013).

10 David Wroe 'First Australian suicide bomber in Iraq reportedly kills three people in Baghdad' 18 July 2014. The Sydney Morning Herald, http://www.smh.com.au/federal-politics/political-news/first-australian-suicide-bomber-in-iraq-reportedly-kills-three-people-in-baghdad–20140718–3c4oe.html#ixzz39QclFlwn (accessed 22 July 2014).

7

Conclusion – Defining the human

At the time of writing this Conclusion, the Australian government has officially raised its terrorist threat level to 'high'; the highest the country has experienced since 9/11. 'What we do have is intelligence that there are people with the intent and the capability to mount attacks,' the Prime Minister, Tony Abbott, said.[1] In a previous speech on 21 August 2014, Mr Abbott invited Australians to join 'Team Australia' in the fight against terrorism and accept new controversial anti-terrorist legislation, which, as we have seen, many Australian Muslims perceive as being aimed at them. The result was that a few days later the Islamic Council of Victoria (ICV), which represents up to 150,000 Muslims, decided to boycott Mr Abbott's meeting with Muslim leaders in Melbourne, which was called to explain the new anti-terrorist legislation and receive feedback from the Muslim community. It is beyond doubt that many Muslims in Australia reacted to Mr Abbott's slogan negatively. Far from alone in his thoughts, Yusuf, a 23-year-old Australian of Lebanese heritage, observed,

> He said that we must joint Team Australia and then that we should not migrate to this country unless we want to join Team Australia. I can say that there is no doubt, Gabriele, that he was speaking about Muslims, both migrants and Australians like me. He says: integrate or fuck off. Team Australia is nothing else than Team Christianity, and I am sorry I am only for Team Islam. There is a deep difference between Team Australia and Team Islam. There are differences in values, morals and respect for God's Law which this country does not have.

Yusuf's reaction and view is not isolated; quite the opposite, in fact. Immediately after the Australian prime minister used the 'Team Australia' phrase, Facebook and Twitter were filled with Muslim protestations, criticisms, sarcastic replies, and even offensive language. Of course, the notion of 'Team Australia' was also criticized by non-Muslims who saw the prime minister's words as nothing less than Islamophobia or as an attack on the Australian doctrine of multiculturalism. On the other hand, other Australians supported the Australian prime minister and expressed their concerns through newspapers and other mass media that Australian Muslims were not doing enough to distance themselves from terrorist organizations such as IS and al-Qaida. A relevant number of comments questioned whether Australian Muslims were compatible with 'the Australian way of life' and Australian values. At the same time the hashtag #MuslimApologies started to gain momentum on Twitter. With this hashtag, Muslims wanted to show that they felt they should not apologize for the actions of certain individuals and groups committing atrocities and terrorizing non-Muslims and Muslims alike. To do so, they used the hashtag to sarcastically apologize for a number of trivial, inconsequential things. An influential imam and Muslim leader in Sydney, however, pointed out an important fact about these feelings among Muslims when he said, 'You see, Muslims in this country, but I expect in other western countries too, are frustrated with being associated with the actions of violent extremists that are committed abroad and then asked to condemn those actions again and again when we even do so more than others.'

Yet, some Muslims are not condemning such acts, quite the opposite: support for IS (formerly ISIS) and other minor terrorist organizations is not so uncommon among young Muslims in particular. Just recently, black flags identical to those used by the Islamic State in Syria and Iraq have been auctioned in a local Sydney mosque.[2] Meanwhile, Wissam Haddad, the controversial head of the al-Risalah Islamic Centre in Sydney's southwest, had no issue to state to a journalist, 'I'm not comfortable personally holding the (Australian) flag because this flag does not represent me as a Muslim. My flag is the flag of Allah. That's my flag. For me to have the Shahada flag, as it's called, that's a flag that I stand and live and die for and I don't stand and live and die for the Australian flag.'[3] Meanwhile, non-Muslim Australians seem increasingly worried about Islam as a religion and all its visible symbols. New plans for mosques in Australia are strongly, and sometimes through clearly racist arguments, opposed, such as in the case of the Bendigo Mosque in Victoria. Behind what may appear to be an objection to the building permit is in reality an anti-Muslim sentiment that goes beyond the building itself. Even a short visit to the Facebook page called 'No Mosque in Bendigo', which has attracted nearly 10,000 members, leaves little doubt about the nature of the opposition, as the mosque plan is rarely discussed and instead the contributions to the page talk of how Islam should not have a place in Australia, perceiving it as an uncivilized religion and against the Australian 'way of life'.[4] Of course, this is not the first time that opposition to mosques and prayer rooms in Western countries are, in reality, attempts to maintain, as an Italian informant of mine said in Milan, 'a de-Muslimised and Shari'a-proof neighbourhood'. This Italian informant went on to explain further: 'You see, if they build the mosque they will mark their territory; there is nothing in common between Muslims and Italians. Islam spreads like that, from mosque to mosque, from minaret to minaret, and one day we will wake up second class citizens under Shari'a law. We need to state a firm "no" to such expansion against Judeo-Christian values' (Marco, 42 year old shop keeper in Milan).

On 17 September 2014, a force of 800 Australian Federal Police, special anti-terrorism units and Australian Security Intelligence Organization (ASIO) raided several homes in the Sydney suburbs. Few were arrested, and at the end only one Muslim was charged with terrorism-related offences. The mass media broadcast videos of Muslims arrested, with their hands behind their backs, sitting on the grass of their front gardens while guarded by heavily armed officers. The plot allegedly involved an intention to kidnap a member of the public and stage a public beheading in IS's style and then broadcast it on Youtube. Fear spread and with it came attacks against Islam as a religion and against Muslims as members of a group. At the same time, lots of Australian Muslims appeared to react defensively against the police raids and anti-terrorist operations. Some of them staged improvised demonstrations where they declared Islam itself to be under attack by the authorities and, with it, Muslims and their culture and civilization.

After observing this, some may pause to wonder whether Huntington (1996) might have been correct in his assumptions. The higher the level of conflict between what many see as the monolithic social-meta-religious entity of the 'West' and the no less monolithic representation of Islam as an ideology, the more the clash of civilizations theory of Huntington may appear to some as somewhat of a fulfilled prophecy. And how can we blame people for assuming that this is the case? In Chapter 2 of this book, I observed that the strong appeal of the clash of civilizations theory, for both ordinary people and leaders, lies in its commonsensical essence. Geertz (1975), as we have seen, has suggested that common sense has some universal characteristics, which he defines as semi-qualities: naturalness, practicalness, thinness, immethodicalness and accessibleness, with naturalness being the most prominent. The role of the mass media in the process of making the clash of civilizations theory popular, especially in ensuring the 'accessibleness' of the clash of civilizations idea, is definitely significant. Unsurprisingly, Mr Abbott has followed the same path of other leaders, such as David Cameron and Angela Merkel, and advocated the assimilation of Muslims, in particular, within a national system of values, which may be read as another way of saying Western civilizational values. The 'Team Australia' phrase is part of the rhetoric of the clash of civilizations, and as such is deeply commonsensical to many ordinary Australians. The complex cultural specifics of Muslim immigrants to Australia and the many generations of Muslim Australians, together with their economic and social realities, have been ignored, just as they were in the United Kingdom and other parts of Europe (Marranci 2008), and, although in a different way, in the United States (Cesari 2013; Kundnani 2012). Yet, civilizational common sense is also found among the different Muslim communities. In this case, it is expressed in terms of the 'Team Islam' rhetoric: Islam is under attack, Islamophobia is the ordinary condition met by Muslims in everyday interactions, the 'flag of Islam' is antithetical to 'the flag of Australia' (or any other Western nation). Hence, instead of a clash of civilization, I have suggested that we should understand the current conflictual situation as a clash of common sense between similar, parallel yet opposite, ways of thinking that in both cases remain more often than not a 'pensée unique'.

In Chapter 2, we have also observed that the concept of *civilization* has its own history both in the non-Muslim West and among Muslim communities and such history is different but significant. *The West* that we read in the mass media, that we hear in politicians' speeches or mentioned in the mosque during a sermon, is not the West as a geographical or even geopolitical entity; rather *The West* is part of civilizational common sense vocabulary. The very idea of *The West* provides a tool to hierarchically differentiate between cultures and human societies (Bonnett 2004). Civilization is no longer a philosophical concept or a convenient label. Civilization, as Starobinski (1993: 30) observes, has become a criterion, where people have to take the side of civilization and are called to 'adopt' its cause and reject what is perceived to threaten the civilization, which inevitably will be tagged as the 'absolute evil'. The rhetoric of *evil* became central in the aftermath of 9/11. With the collapse of the Twin Towers, a powerful symbol was created: the symbol of the endangered civilization, of that Western civilisation which, as we have seen, represents rationality itself against the brutality of the uncivilized. The imagination of the Muslim as the archetypical threat to civilization is not something new, as indeed even an eighteenth-century philosopher such as Voltaire in his *Le fanatisme, ou Mahomet le Prophete* represented Islam as an anti-Enlightenment, anti-civilization force, and he is just one of many historical examples.

Although Huntington's theory suffers, as discussed in Chapter 2, from flawed essentialism, any honest analysis of the current tensions existing between Muslim communities and non-Muslims would have to admit that the tensions are often perceived, felt and imagined through the prism of civilizational rhetoric and ideas. However, it would be no less essentialist to suggest that entire groups perceive the current conflict in such a way. Indeed, discussing 'communities' or 'groups' or even Muslims and non-Muslims in general terms may not be helpful in clarifying the dynamics of such a conflict.

I have suggested that instead we can focus on the individual and those who share particular visions of 'values' and how they relate to discourses of 'how to be human'. I have decided to use the term civilizer in this book to identify such *forma mentis*. In other words, I have suggested that what we are observing is the result of a cognitive process that brings certain individuals to look at others through their own narrative of civilization. As we have discussed, behind this process there is the fear that other groups may alienate, threaten or dilute one's own values and their purity (Douglas 1988). The civilizers' wars are not only fought on the battlefield, that is, through suicide bombings and other acts of terrorism or through anti-terrorist retaliations, drones and other violent means, but are also fought in more subtle ways, often in everyday dynamics of power, which are based on narratives, rhetoric and labels that aim to discredit and devalue that which is considered uncivilized, in the process asserting one's own values.

In Chapter 3, I have noticed that anthropological studies of Muslims, Islam and politics often appear to have overlooked an important dynamic: the fact that everyday interactions include not only the conceptual categories of 'Islam' and 'Muslim' but also the inevitable ones of 'non-Muslim' and 'non-Islam'. Even in ethnography, it is hard to find such interaction explained or analytically dissected – with the exception, perhaps, of Rabinow (1997), who, however, did so through an emotional personal experience (See Marranci 2008). The reason for such lack of attention to the relationship between the above categories may be found in the fact that, till today, the study of Muslims is not the study of humans who identify themselves as 'Muslims' but rather the study of people as cultural symbols, as expressions of a "religion" instead of as the embodiers of religion. In other words, what I had called 'the fallacy of the "Muslim mind theory"' (Marranci 2008: 6) remains, latently or explicitly, detectable in many studies. 'The Muslim' is a category to be explained instead of a human with emotions, feelings and cognitive processes. This becomes more so, as we have seen in Chapter 6, when concepts such as 'jihad' or even the vague 'Islamic terrorism' are debated or researched. The understanding of Islam and Muslims as 'cultural' categories has facilitated the development of what I have named the *dichotomic synecdoches*: modernism/scripturalism, secularism/fundamentalism, democracy/sharia. This selection of a part for the all (i.e. synecdoche) is central to the ontology of the civilizer's rhetoric. Recently, there have been some attempts to introduce new concepts such as *Islam mondain*, which aim to make scholars focus on what Muslims phenomenologically do in their interaction with their environment, in particular, in the context of secular democracies. Although this may help, we have seen in Chapter 3 that, at the same time, we need to acknowledge that many Muslims find the concept of the secular problematic. The issue is the civilizers' perception that their own civilization has been contaminated and is in a stage of decadence.

Both Muslims and non-Muslims, should they become overly focused on such ontology of culture, may become civilizers themselves; however, how this transformation manifests itself in an individual is variable.

Labels and stereotypes, as we have discussed in Chapter 3, are an essential part in the process of stigmatization, which is one of the essential tools in the hands of civilizers. Another central concept that we have highlighted is that of 'ethos' or, rather, the perceived lack of it in whoever is considered to be an obstacle to the supremacy of one's own values. Ethos, framed and defined through the values of civilization, is at the end, according to civilizers, what defines who is human, and consequently who can be treated as such. I have suggested that contemporary civilizers, mutatis mutandis, are no different to their progenitors in that their rhetoric is ultimately centred on the discourse of *ethos*. In Chapter 3, I have provided an analysis of how we can understand 'ethos' in such a context and described how the ultimate goal of any civilizer, although the methodology may differ as much as the narrative, is that of defining the *ethos* of their own group and, in doing so, to define who is properly 'human'. In extreme cases, the civilizer's rhetoric, or even violence, may be directed against his or her own group because of a perception of it as being responsible for a betrayal of 'ethos', with the violence being the last attempt to 'reawaken' the correct group ethos, as we have observed in the actions of terrorist Anders Behring Breivik in Norway.

But in what ways are the civilizers' narratives formed and expressed? In Chapter 4, I have noticed that although the research and academic literature on Islamophobia, and even more on orientalism, is today rather developed, so that most of the stereotyping of Muslims is well presented and debated, the same cannot be said about the stereotypes that some Muslims develop about the West both in Muslim-majority countries as well as in Western countries. Buruma and Margalit (2004) called such stereotypes concerning the West 'Occidentalism'. As we have seen, very few other scholars (and at present no anthropologists as far as I can trace) have, after them, researched the topic. Occidentalism among some extremist Islamic groups or individuals seems to be the product of a loop. As Aydin (2006) has suggested, the narrative developed by postcolonial theories developed in the 1960–1970s fed the more recent narratives of the latter Islamic groups, which had assimilated the modern anti-imperialist discourse and, as in the case of the 1979 Iranian Revolution, integrated it into a religious revolutionary discourse. The impact that postcolonial and postmodern theories have had on Muslim occidentalism was revealed also by my own research in Australia where a certain Fanonian (1963, 1970) understanding of relations between Muslims and non-Muslims is expressed by some.

We have also observed another aspect that has been understudied, but which is central to the topic of this book: conspiracism. Again, if most of the conspiracy theories concerning Islam and Muslims are well known and studied, the same cannot be said about conspiracy theories reported, developed and discussed by Muslims. Works like, for instance, Pipes's (1996, 1997), despite surely being pioneering, suffer from what Stempel et. al have identified as a pathological approach, in which the issue, again, is the Arab or Muslim 'mind'. Furthermore, even this limited – in quality and analysis – literature (Gray 2008) focuses on Arab and Muslim-majority countries. The study of the impact that conspiracism may have on the conceptualization of the 'West' among Muslims born and raised in Western countries remains still a rather neglected field of research; however, as I have suggested in Chapter 4, this research would be very relevant considering the recent wars of terror, which have seen a proliferation of parallel and opposing conspiracy theories.

As we have discussed above, ethos is central to the civilizers' development of ontologies and *jahiliyya* is a concept that appears, directly or indirectly, in occidentalist rhetoric. The West is considered by some to be pure *jahiliyya* and so thought to pose a threat to Islam. Although some Muslims who use the concept may have read Mawdudi's and Qutb's work, the majority of my informants did not know this work very well, although they still clearly expressed the conviction that the influence of Western culture corrupts the practice of Islam, and liberal Islam is often the result of this process. The main point in this discourse is that the West, including its democracy and legal system, is inherently 'a-just', or in other words, a product of *jahiliyya*. Justice, as we have seen in this book, is an essential element of the confrontation between civilizers in the current wars of terror. It is no surprise that so much discussion and antagonism exists around a rather complex and legalistic concept such as sharia. For the non-Muslim civilizers, sharia is the ultimate expression of barbarism, the deadly poison that, given a chance, would reduce the Judeo-Christian civilization to a state of 'dhimmitude'. An Australian senator, Jacqui Lambie, on 22 September 2014, declared that sharia 'involves terrorism' and 'I just think sharia law you get it mixed up. ... If you're going to be a supporter of sharia law, and you're not going to support our constitution and an allegiance to our constitution and Australian law, then um ...'[5] It is clear that for the senator, sharia is a danger to the 'values' of Western society. For some Muslims, it is the Western legal system that is perceived to be a threat to real justice: the law of God. Of course, it is not difficult to see how both the parallel fears of sharia and Judeo-Christian jahiliyya feed the minds and ideas of those ready to defend their own side of 'civilization' and how those minds tautologically reinforce their own convictions through conspiracy theories. The counterposed conspiracy theories are the result of the fear that an external threat might change, alter or in particular annihilate one's 'way of life', which, of course, civilizers consider the only correct way to be 'human'.

Gender, as we have discussed in Chapter 5, is a central focus of the civilizers' clash. Nothing has attracted more vitriolic exchanges between, on the one hand, those who see the West as the pinnacle of civilization and Islam as its barbaric opposite and, on the other hand, those who hold just the opposite view, more than the conduct of women and, more recently, the condition or the very existence of non-heterosexuals. The fight (unfortunately not always metaphorical) about who has freed women from oppression is not a recent one. In Chapter 5, we have observed how the European colonial endeavour has been often justified through the alleged pursuit of gender equity and the liberation of women from barbaric oppression, including what the colonizers (such as the French in Algeria, for instance) saw as oppression that was the product of Islam. At that time, Enlightenment and the narrative of civilizing women offered the European colonial powers the moral justification they needed. As I have highlighted in the chapter, after 9/11 and the US decision to invade Afghanistan, the rhetoric of freeing Muslim women from their religious oppressors appeared again. For instance, we have seen how Laura Bush hoped that the War on Terror would fight for the rights and dignity of women – not just in Afghanistan, since she implied that if Islamic terrorism was not stopped, the horrible condition of Afghan women may one day be shared by Western women too.

As we have seen, even feminists showed their favour for the ban in Europe of the burqa and the niqab, both veils which cover a woman's face, in the name of liberating women from oppression. Today in Australia, the debate over banning these dress items has been reopened by Prime Minister Tony Abbott who defined them as confrontational and affirmed that he would have preferred women not to wear them.[6] Recently, movements such as Femen have clearly used civilizers' rhetoric, and also the bodies of its members to attract public attention to what they perceive as the oppression of Islam of women. The focus on clothing, or lack of it, is not a new discourse; evaluations of civilization have often been in some way associated with clothing and how much skin a woman is able to reveal in public (Oliver 2013).

Yet, if the anti-Muslim rhetoric of those who believe themselves to be the defenders of the Judeo-Christian civilization is again well represented, analysed and discussed in academic literature, the same cannot be said of the rhetoric of those among Muslims who perceive a woman in a mini-skirt as an attack on Islam or, as infamously Seik Taj el-Din al-Hilali said, 'uncovered meat', and hence responsible for inciting rape. In other words, a book similar to Kahf's *Western representations of Muslim woman: From termagant to odalisque* (1999) has yet to be written, at least in the English language. Although the literature is still lacking, we have observed how this rhetoric of gender indeed exists among some Muslims living in both Western and Muslim-majority nations. As we have seen in Chapter 5, we can observe that some Muslim groups, particularly after 9/11, have increased their efforts to 'save' non-Muslim women from the decadent culture of the West and its objectification of women.

Women are not the only ones often deemed in need of salvation, however, as we can observe another dynamic of gender between civilizers. Some will point out that Islam is dangerous not only to women but also to gays and lesbians, along with anyone else who does not conform to heteronormative standards. Yet, some others claim that homosexuality is one of the most poisonous products of the West, to the extent that one can hear even the expression 'Western disease' to refer to it. In other words, if some Judeo-Christian civilizers want to save gays from Islam, some Muslim civilizers want to save Islam from gays. As we have discussed in the chapter, the fear of the impact that homosexuality may have on Muslims is linked to the fear that civilizers have of 'liberal Islam': both of these, of course, are not just products of the West but are instead seen as actual weapons intended to disrupt Islam. Again, fear and conspiracy theories help some to perceive changes in legislation that not only decriminalizes homosexuality but actually extends rights, such as marriage, to non-heterosexuals, as well as allowing public events such as gay pride parades, as the ultimate evidence that the West is corrupt and a threat to young Muslims. Indeed, in the narrative of would-be Muslim civilizers, the West – always seen as 'Christian' even when secular – is the land of corruption and hedonism, while 'Islam' is reduced to a religion of abstinence, honour, sacrifice (if not martyrdom) and courage, at least in their cognitive representation of it.

Recent civilizers' discourse on gender has not been limited to clothes and sexual preferences, but extends to who 'takes' the women of whom. Increasingly, in the aftermath of 9/11, there has been an unusual level of concern about who women are seeing, making love with and, in particular, about who may exploit them. The fear that foreigners may take women from local men is not a new one and even a well-known Roman legend reminds us so. Yet, new urban legends, or rather misreadings of ordinary crimes, have resuscitated the image of the Saracen kidnapping the Christian woman for the Sultan's harem. In the UK, but also in Australia and Canada, reports of 'Muslim gangs' grooming young, vulnerable white teenagers for sex or prostitution have hit the headlines of newspapers and have, of course, spread to blogs, some of which are clear in their mission to increase hatred against Muslims. Some civilizers have represented such incidents as being further argument to show how barbaric Muslims are and how dangerous they are to women. Of course, it did not matter that those cases were very few, nor that the South Asians involved were nominal Muslims. The resulting fear and conspiracy theories are spread and used to convince others that Islam, and so Muslims, are a danger to how we are humans.

However, as we know, this is not a one-way street, and among Muslim communities, we may find similar, parallel but opposite, ideas. For example, many Muslims would consider it unacceptable for a Muslim woman to marry a non-Muslim man. Feeding off this viewpoint, the fear that public schools with coeducational classes could pose a 'danger' to Muslim girls has become a trope among some groups and Muslim individuals who campaign for the necessity of enrolling young people in single-sex classes. Sadly, some Muslim girls have paid with their lives for breaking religious and cultural norms as far as sex rules are concerned. Although the great majority of Muslims living in Western countries condemn what is labelled with the general term 'honour killings', it is undeniable that among a minority of Muslims such killings, or related beatings or psychological tortures, are at least justified in the name of preserving the 'Islamic way of life' that they fear is threatened.

In Chapter 6, we observed and discussed why some civilizers may move from rhetoric to actual acts of violence, or to specific acts of terrorism. We had already discussed the case of the white supremacist and self-defined crusader Anders Behring Breivik, who explained his actions as a desperate attempt to save his 'civilization'. We have other examples, such as the less-known Roberto Sandalo who, with a group of supporters in Italy, planned and was on his way to execute a number of terrorist attacks against local mosques and even a Muslim school.[7] Although the decision to perform an act of terrorism in the name of a religion or an ideal is not new and, of course, existed before 9/11, recent incidents demonstrate deep differences with some previous cases, such as the case of the Red Brigades (Meade 1990). In this chapter, we have discussed the case of Younes Tsouli, also better known as Irhabi 007, who I knew during my research. I have suggested that emotions have an important role to play in particular in the case of terrorism organized by Muslims born and raised in Western countries and in incidents involving someone who has been often called the lone wolf. In this chapter, I have suggested a theoretical framework that, starting from the neurologist Damasio's views on emotions, combines Agnew's general strain theory with recent research on cognitive dissonance. It is my contention that this theoretical framework explains what I have defined as emotional Islam (Marranci 2009). As we have seen, the term emotional Islam identifies a process by which Islam is not experienced as a religion dependent upon a particular theology and theological discourses that are historical in origin and linked to traditions, but rather as independent values or, in other words, as an ontologised 'ethos'.

Of course, as I have explained in my previous works (Marranci 2006, 2008), it would be wrong to consider as 'non-Islam' certain radical views of Islam, since for that person, his or her understanding of it is the *real* Islam and the only way to be Muslim, or at least the best way of being so. Hence, emotional Islam is not a term that seeks to differentiate between 'real Islam' and something else that is less real, or even wrong. As I have explained elsewhere, as soon as we try to classify Islam, we leave the analytical field and enter a theological or apologetical domain. As such, emotional Islam identifies a phenomenological way of being Muslim. A common aspect of emotional Islam is the essentialization of the idea of justice, where justice becomes unmediated and an emotional category, rather than, as in other views of Islam, a result of being Muslim. It is no surprise that emotional Islam can be observed among many young Muslims living in Western countries. It is beyond question that they are exposed to injustices and abuses of their identity, as Muslims or as part of an ethnic group, more than other members of mainstream society. The event of 9/11 added further pressure to young people, and anti-terrorism laws, like those recently introduced in Australia, have only exacerbated this sense of injustice and facilitated emotional Islam and in some cases, along with it, a strong civilization rhetoric.

I started this book suggesting that what has been called the 'War on Terror' should be perceived as 'wars of terror', in which the main fighters are those whom, for convenience, I have described as civilizers. Although Huntington (1996) had correctly identified the challenges that the post-Cold War world had to face, he focused on an essentialized idea of religion as civilization. He was right in identifying the concept of civilization as central, but wrong in his analysis of its role. Indeed, we do not have a clash of civilizations, which, in such terms, phenomenologically does not exist, but rather a clash among opposing, but similar, ways of thinking. We have a clash of civilizers, in which individual humans, rather than solely cultural dynamics, matter. Huntington's thesis cannot explain why not all Muslims or all Christians or all Confucians support the clash other than assuming that those who do not take part in this conflict of cultures are not real representatives of their respective civilizational corners. In observing instead a clash of civilizers, we have a specific way of understanding and making sense of the surrounding world that can be particular to individuals. This is the reason this book has explored some of the rhetoric used by civilizers and even the reasons why some of this rhetoric will remain at the level of rhetoric instead of becoming actual, violent action.

We live in an increasingly polarized world where wars of terror are advocated, perceived, imagined or actually suffered. In particular for young people, who tend to be more subjected to emotions and hence feelings, the temptation to find security in the strong identities of civilizers is great. In recent events that derive from this new phase of terrorism – the establishment of IS or the more unusual, but probably, in future, more common example of Breivik, we can witness the spread of the wars of terror.

If my assumption is correct – that the spiral of violence that we are witnessing globally today, marked by a circle of panic, feeds the existence of those whom I have named civilizers, inspires their rhetoric and allows them to reinforce their emotional call to the defence of one or the other ways of life – then the only way of ensuring that we do not remain trapped within the wars of terror is to stop this circle of panic.

Notes

1 Emma Griffiths 'Terrorism threat: Australian alert level raised to high; terrorist attack likely but not imminent' ABC, 11 September 2014, http://www.abc.net.au/news/2014-09-12/australia-increases-terrorism-threat-level/5739466 (accessed 8 October 2014).

2 M. Godfrey and L. Van Den Broeke 'Hate for sale as Muslim flag adopted by jihadists goes to auction at Sydney mosque' 8 September 2014, http://www.dailytelegraph.com.au/news/nsw/hate-for-sale-as-muslim-flag-adopted-by-jihadists-goes-to-auction-at-sydney-mosque/story-fni0cx12–1227050847756 (accessed 8 October 2014).

3 M. Godfrey and L. Van Den Broeke 'Islam in Australia: Living and dying for the flag of Allah' 19 September 2014, http://www.dailytelegraph.com.au/news/nsw/islam-in-australia-living-and-dying-for-the-flag-of-allah/story-fni0cx12–1227028712490 (accessed 8 October 2014).

4 http://www.facebook.com/pages/Stop-the-Mosque-in-Bendigo (accessed 8 October 2014).

5 Geoff Egan 'Anti-Sharia Senator Lambie unable to say what Sharia is' The Queensland Times http://www.qt.com.au/news/Anti-Sharia-Senator-Jacqui-Lambie-unable-define-it/2393960/ (accessed 8 October 2014).

6 http://www.radioaustralia.net.au/international/2014–10–01/prime-minister-tony-abbott-reveals-he-wishes-the-burka-was-not-worn-in-australia/1374493 (accessed 8 October 2014).

7 See http://www1.adnkronos.com/AKI/English/Security/?id=3.0.2804874580 (accessed 8 October 2014).

References

Abbas, T. (2007), 'Muslim minorities in Britain: Integration, multiculturalism and radicalism in the post–7/7 period', *Journal of Intercultural Studies*, 28(3): 287–300.

Abraham, I. (2008), '"Sodomized by religion": Fictional representations of Queer Muslims in the West', *Topia: Canadian Journal of Cultural Studies*, 19: 137–52.

Abraham, I. (2009), 'Out to get us': Queer Muslims and the clash of sexual civilisations in Australia', *Contemporary Islam*, 3(1): 79–97.

Abu-Lughod, L. (2002), 'Do Muslim women really need saving? Anthropological reflections on cultural relativism and its others', *American Anthropologist*, 104(3): 783–90.

Abu-Lughod, L. (2013), *Do Muslim Women Need Saving?* Cambridge, MA: Harvard University Press.

Adler, F. and Laufer, W. S., eds (1995), A*dvances in Criminological Theory. Vol. 10, The Legacy of Anomie Theory*, New Brunswick, NJ: Transaction.

Agnew, R. (1985), 'A revised strain theory of delinquency', *Social Forces*, 64: 151–67.

Agnew, R. (1989), 'A longitudinal test of revised strain theory', *Journal of Quantitative Criminology*, 5: 373–88.

Agnew, R. (1992), 'Foundation for a general strain theory of crime and delinquency', *Criminology*, 30: 47–88.

Agnew, R. (2001), 'Building on the foundation of general strain theory: Specifying the types of strain most likely to lead to crime and delinquency', *Journal of Research in Crime and Delinquency*, 38: 319–61.

Agnew, R. (2006), *Pressured into Crime: An Overview of General Strain Theory*, Los Angeles: Roxbury.

Agnew, R. (2010), 'A general strain theory of terrorism', *Theoretical Criminology*, 14(2): 131–53.

Agnew, R. and White, H. (1992), 'An empirical test of general strain theory', *Criminology*, 30: 475–500.

Aimé-Martin, L. (1843), *The Education of Mothers: Or the Civilization of Mankind by Women*, trans. Edwin Lee, Philadelphia and Chicago: Lea & Blanchard.

Alasuutari, P. (2004), 'The principles of Pax Americana', *Cultural Studies Critical Methodologies*, 4(2): 246–9.

Allen, C. (2010), *Islamophobia*, Chicago: Ashgate Publishing, Ltd.

Allen, C. (2011), 'Opposing Islamification or promoting Islamophobia? Understanding the english defence league', *Patterns of Prejudice*, 45(4): 279–94.

Almond, G. A., Appleby, R. S. and Sivan, E. (2003), *Strong Religion: The Rise of Fundamentalisms Around the World*, Chicago and London: University of Chicago Press.

Asad, M. (2004), *The Message of the Qur'an*, Bristol: The Book Foundations.

Asad, T. (2003), *Formations of the Secular: Christianity, Islam, Modernity*, Stanford: Stanford University Press.

Aseltine, R. H., Gore, S. and Gordon, J. (2000), 'Life stress, anger and anxiety, and delinquency: An empirical test of general strain theory', *Journal of Health and Social Behavior*, 41: 256–75.

Aupers, S. (2012), '"Trust no one": Modernization, paranoia and conspiracy culture', *European Journal of Communication*, 27(1): 22–34.

Aydemir, M. (2012), 'Dutch homonationalism and intersectionality', *The Postcolonial Low Countries: Literature, Colonialism, and Multiculturalism*, 178–202.

Aydin, C. (2006), 'Between Occidentalism and the global left: Islamist critiques of the West in Turkey', *Comparative Studies of South Asia, Africa and the Middle East*, 26(3): 446–61.

Ayubi, N. (1997), 'Islam and democracy', in David Potter, David Goldblatt, Margaret Kiloh and Paul Lewis (eds), *Democratization*, 345–62, Cambridge, MA: Polity Press.

Bangstad, S. (2009), 'Contesting secularism/s Secularism and Islam in the work of Talal Asad', *Anthropological Theory*, 9(2): 188–208.

Bao, H. (2013), 'A Jihad for love, by Parvez Sharma: (director). Run time: 81 minutes. Produced by Sandi Dubowski and Parvez Sharma, 2008 (released May 21, 2008). $24.95 DVD', *Journal of Homosexuality*, 60(5): 796–800.

Bao, W., Haas, A. and Pi, Y. (2004), 'Life strain, negative emotions, and delinquency: An empirical test of general strain theory in the People's Republic of China', *International Journal of Offender Therapy and Comparative Criminology*, 48: 281–97.

Bar-Tal, D. (2000), *Shared Beliefs in a Society: Social Psychological Analysis*, Thousand Oaks, CA: Sage.

Barazangi, N. H., Zaman, M. R. and Afzal, O., eds (1996), *Islamic Identity and the Struggle for Justice*, Gainesville: University Press of Florida.

Baron, S. W. (2004), 'General strain, street youth and crime: A test of Agnew's revised theory', *Criminology*, 42: 457–83.

Bateson, G. (1936), *Naven*, Cambridge: Cambridge University Press.

Bateson, G. (2002), *Mind and Nature*, Creskill, NJ: Hampton Press.

Beecher, J. (1990), *Charles Fourier: The Visionary and his World*, Berkeley: University of California Press.

Beg, M. A. (1982), *Islamic and Western Concepts of Civilization*, Kuala Lumpur: The University of Malaya Press.

Benlahcene, B. (2004), 'Civilization in the Western and Islamic cultural traditions: A conceptual historical approach', in A. Long, J. Awang and K. Salleh (eds), *Islam: Past, Present and Future*, 912–23, Selangor: University Kebangsaan Malaysia Bangi.

Ben-Ze'ev, A. (2000), *The Subtlety of Emotions*, Cambridge, MA: MIT Press.

Berger, P. L., Berger, B. and Kellner, H. (1973), *The Homeless Mind: Modernization and Consciousness*, New York: Random House.

Bhabha, H. (1994), *The Location of Culture*, London and New York: Routledge.

Bhabha, H. (2001), 'In a spirit of calm violence', in G. Prakash (ed.), *After Colonialism: Imperial Histories and Postcolonial Displacements*, 326–43, Princeton: Princeton University Press.

Bilgrami, A. (2006), 'Occidentalism, the very idea: An essay on enlightenment and enchantment', *Critical Inquiry*, 32(3): 381–411.

Billig, M. (1987), *Arguing and Thinking: A Rhetorical Approach to Social Psychology*, Cambridge: Cambridge University Press.

bin Laden, O., Lawrence, B. B. and Howarth, J. (2005), *Messages to the World: The Statements of Osama Bin Laden*, London: Verso.

Bock, G. (2002), *Women in European History*, Oxford: Blackwell.

Boddy, J. P. (2007), *Civilizing Women: British Crusades in Colonial Sudan*, Princeton: Princeton University Press.

Boltanski, L. and Chiapello, E. (2005), *The New Spirit of Capitalism*, London: Verso.

Bonnett, A. (2004), *The Idea of the West: Culture, Politics, and History*, Basingstoke: Palgrave Macmillan.

Bonney, R. (2004), *Jihad: From Qur'an to bin Laden*. London: Palgrave Macmillan.

Bourdieu, P. (1987), 'What makes a social class? On the theoretical and practical existence of groups', *Berkeley Journal of Sociology*, 32: 1–18.

Bourdieu, P. (1990), *The Logic of Practice*, Stanford, CA: Stanford University Press.

Bowden, B. (2004), 'Theideal of civilisation: Its origins and socio-political character', *Critical Review of International Social and Political Philosophy*, 7(1): 25–50.

Bowden, B. (2007), 'Civilization and savagery in the Crucible of war', *Peace Research Abstracts Journal*, 44 (4): 3.

Bracke, S. (2012), 'From "saving women" to "saving gays": Rescue narratives and their dis/continuities', *European Journal of Women's Studies*, 19(2): 237–52.

Braudel, F. (1994), *A History of Civilizations*, New York: A. Lane.

Brenner, S. (1996), 'Reconstructing self and society: Javanese Muslim women and "the veil"', *American Ethnologist*, 23: 673–97.

Broidy, L. M. (2001), 'A test of general strain theory', *Criminology*, 39(1): 9–36.

Brosnan, S. F. (2006), 'Nonhuman species' reactions to inequity and their implications for fairness', *Social Justice Research*, 19: 153–85.

Brotherton, R. (2013), 'Towards a definition of "conspiracy theory"', *Psychology Postgraduate Affairs Groups*, 88: 9–14.

Bulliet, R. W. (2004), *The Case for Islamo-Christian Civilization,* New York: Columbia University Press.

Bunt, G. (2009), *iMuslims: Rewiring the house of Islam,*Chapel Hill, NC: University of North Carolina Press.

Burton, A. M. (1990), 'The white Woman's burden: British feminists and the Indian Woman, 1865–1915', *Women's Studies International Forum*, 13(4): 295–308.

Buruma, I. and Margalit, A. (2004), *Occidentalism: A Short History of Anti-westernism*, London: Atlantic Books.

Butler, L. D., Koopman, C. and Zimbardo, P. G. (1995), 'The psychological impact of viewing the film JFK: Emotions, beliefs, and political behavioural intentions', *Political Psychology*, 16(2): 237–57.

Buunk, B. P. and Schaufeli, W. B. (1999), 'Reciprocity in interpersonal relationships: An evolutionary perspective on its importance for health and well-being', *European Review of Social Psychology*, 10: 259–91.

Byford, J. (2011), *Conspiracy Theories: A Critical Introduction*, London: Palgrave Macmillan.

Campbell, C (2007), *The Easternization of the West: A Thematic Account of Cultural Change in the Modern Era*, Boulder, CO: Paradigm Publishers.

Casanova, J. (2005), 'Catholic and Muslim politics in comparative perspective', *Taiwan Journal of Democracy*, 1(2): 89–108.

Casanova, J. (2011), 'Cosmopolitanism, the clash of civilizations and multiple modernities', *Current Sociology*, 59(2): 252–67.

Cesari, J. (2013), 'The so-called failure of multiculturalism: A securitization approach', *In 20th International Conference of Europeanists-Crisis & Contingency: States of (In) Stability*, Council for European Studies, Columbia University, Tuesday, 25 June 2013.

Chalk, F. and Jonassohn, K. (1990), 'The history and sociology of genocide: Analyses and case studies', New Haven, CT: Yale University Press.

Chestler, P. (2010), 'Worldwide trends in Honor killings', *Middle East Quaterly*, 17: 3–11.

Chua B. H. (2003), 'Multiculturalism in Singapore: An instrument of social control', *Race & Class*, 44(3): 58–77.

Cockbain, E. (2013), 'Grooming and the "Asian sex gang predator": The construction of a racial crime threat', *Race & Class*, 54(4): 22–32.

Cockburn, P. and Verso (2015), *The Rise of Islamic State: ISIS and the New Sunni Revolution*, London: Verso.

Cohen, S. (2011), 'Whose side were we on? The undeclared politics of moral panic theory', *Crime, Media, Culture*, 7(3): 237–43.

Collet, T. (2009), 'Civilization and civilized in post-9/11 US presidential speeches', *Discourse & Society*, 20(4): 455–75.

Collier, J. F. (1994), 'Interwined histories: Islamic law and western imperialism', *Law & Soc'y Rev*, 28: 395.

Cook, D. (2005), *Understanding Jihad*, Los Angeles and London: University of California Press.

Cooke, M. (2002), 'Islamic Feminism before and after September 11th', *Duke Journal of Gender Law and Policy*, 9: 227–35.

Corera (2008), Online news story, http://news.bbc.co.uk/2/hi/7191248.stm.

Cosmides, L. and Tooby, J. (2000), 'Evolutionary psychology and the emotions', in M. Lewis and J. M. Haviland-Jones (eds), *Handbook of Emotions*, 91–115, New York: Guilford Press.

Croft, S. (2006), *Culture, Crisis and America's War on Terror*, Cambridge: Cambridge University Press.

Cropanzano, R., Stein, J. H. and Nadisic, T. (2010), *Social Justice and the Experience of Emotion*, Oxford, UK: Taylor & Francis.

Damasio, A. R. (2003), 'Mental self: The person within', *Nature*, 423: 227.

Damasio, A. R. (2004), *Looking for Spinoza: Joy, Sorrow and the Feeling Brain*, London: Vintage.

Darwin, H., Neave, N. and Holmes, J. (2011), 'Belief in conspiracy theories. The role of paranormal belief, paranoid ideation, and schizotypy', *Personality and Individual Differences*, 50: 1289–93.

de Waal, F. (1996), *Good Natured: The Origins of Right and Wrong in Humans and Other Animals*, Cambridge, MA: Harvard University Press.

Delphy, C. (2015), *Dominating Others: Feminism and Racism after the War on Terror*, London: Verso.

Devereux, G. (1980), *Basic problems of ethnopsychiatry,* Chicago: University of Chicago Press.

Dimaggio, A. R. (2008), *Mass Media, Mass Propaganda: Examining American News in the War on Terror,* Lanham, MD: Lexington Books.

Dixon, W. W., ed. (2004), *Film and Television After September 11,* Carbondale: Southern Illinois University Press.

Douglas, M. (1988), 'Purity and danger: An analysis of the concepts of pollution and taboo', London: Ark Paperbacks.

Durham, M. (2015), *American Conservatism and the War on Terror,* London: Routledge.

Eickelman, D. F. and Piscatori, J. P. (2004), *Muslim Politics,* Princeton: Princeton University Press.

Elias, N. (1978), *The Civilizing Process,* New York: Urizen Books.

Eltantawy, N. (2013), 'The veil', in Cynthia Carter, Linda Steiner and Lisa McLaughlin (eds), *The Routledge Companion to Media & Gender,* 384–92, Chicago: Routledge.

Esposito J. L. (1991), *Islam and Politics,* Syracuse: Syracuse University Press.

Esposito, J. L. (1999), *The Islamic Threat: Myth and Reality?* New York: Oxford University Press.

Evans-Pritchard, E. E. (1949), *The Sanusi of Cyrenaica,* Oxford: Clarendon Press.

Fahrenthold, D. A. and Boorstein, M. (2011), 'Rep. Peter King's Muslim Hearings: A key moment in an angry conversation, *Washington Post,* 9, http://www.washingtonpost.com/wp-dyn/content/article/2011/03/09/AR2011030902061.html.

Fallaci, O. (2002), *The Rage and the Pride,* 27, New York: Rizzoli.

Fanon, F. (1963), *The Wretched of the Earth,* New York: Grove Chicago.

Fanon, F. (1970), *Black Skin, White Masks,* Chicago: Paladin.

Faoud, A. (1993), 'The summoning', *Foreign Affairs,* 72(4): 2–9.

Farrington, D. P. (1986), 'Age and crime', *Crime and Justice: An Annual Review of Research,* 7: 189–250.

Featherstone, R. and Deflem, M. (2003), 'Anomie and strain: Context and consequences of Merton's two theories', *Sociological Inquiry,* 73(4): 471–89.

Fekete, L. (2012), 'The Muslim conspiracy theory and the Oslo massacre', *Race & Class,* 53(3): 30–47.

Feldherr, A., ed. (2009), *The Cambridge Companion to the Roman Historians,* Cambridge: Cambridge University Press.

Fernandez, S. (2009), 'The crusade over the bodies of women', *Patterns of Prejudice,* 43(3–4): 269–86.

Festinger, L.(1957), *A Theory of Cognitive Dissonance,* Stanford, CA: Stanford University Press.

Fowler, C. (2007), 'Journalists in feminist clothing: Men and women reporting Afghan women during operation enduring freedom, 2001', *Journal of International Women's Studies,* 8(2): 1–19.

Fox, J. (2001), 'Civilization, religious, and national explanations for ethnic rebellion in the post-cold war middle east', *Jewish Political Studies Review,* 13(2): 177–204.

Franks, B., Bangerter, A. and Bauer, M. W. (2013), 'Conspiracy theories as quasi-religious mentality: An integrated account from cognitive science, social representations theory, and frame theory', *Frontiers in Psychology,* 4: 424–34.

Fuller, R. C. (2007), *Wonder: From Emotion to Spirituality,* Chapel Hill, NC: The University of Carolina Press.

Fullom, S. W. (1855), *The History of Woman, and her Connexion with Religion, Civilization &Domestic Manners from the Earliest Period*, London: Routledge &Co.

Funk, N. C. and Said, A. A. (2004), 'Islam and the West: Narratives of conflict and conflict transformation', *International Journal of Peace Studies*, 9(1): 1–28.

Gadamer, H. G. (1965), *Wahrheit und Methode: Grundzüge einer philosophischen Hermeneutik*, Tübingen: Mohr.

Gaitskell, D. (1998), 'From "Women and imperialism" to gendering colonialism?', *South African Historical Journal*, 39(1): 176–93.

Gallup News Service (2010), In U.S., religious prejudice stronger against Muslims. Retrieved from http://www.gallup.com/poll/125312/Religious-Prejudice-Stronger-Against-Muslims.aspx.

Ganem, N. M. (2010), 'The role of negative emotion in general strain theory', *Journal of Contemporary Criminal Justice*, 26(2): 167–85.

Gaubatz, P. D. and Sperry, P. E. (2009), *Muslim Mafia: Inside the Secret Underworld that's Conspiring to Islamize America*, New York: Wnd Books.

Geertz, C. (1957), 'Ethos, world-view and the analysis of sacred symbols', *The Antioch Review*, 17(4): 421–37.

Geertz, C. (1968), *Islam Observed*, Chicago: University Press.

Geertz, C. (1973), *The Interpretation of Culture*, New York: Basic Books.

Geertz, C. (1975), 'Common sense as a cultural system', *The Antioch Review*, 33(1): 5–26.

Gellner, E (1963), 'Sanctity, puritanism, secularisation and nationalism in North Africa', *Archives de Sociologie des Religions*, 15: 71–86.

Gellner, E. (1968), 'A pendulum swing theory of Islam', *Archives Marocaines de Sociologie*, 1: 5–14.

Gellner, E. (1969), *Saints of the Atlas*, Chicago: University Press.

Gellner, E. (1981), *Muslim Society*, Cambridge: University Press.

Gerges, F.A. (1999), *America and Political Islam: Clash of Cultures or Clash of Interests?* Cambridge: Cambridge University Press.

Gilpin, R. (2005), 'War is too important to be left to ideological amateurs', *International Relations*, 19(1): 5–18.

Gilsenan, M. (1990), 'Very like a camel: The appearance of an anthropologist's Middle East', in R. Fardon (ed.), *Localizing Strategies: Regional Traditions of Ethnographic Writing*, 220–39, Edinburgh: Scottish Academic Press; Washington, DC: Smithsonian Institution Press.

Gleeson, K. (2004), 'From centenary to the Olympics: Gang rape in Sydney', *Current Issues in Criminology*, 16(2): 18–201.

Goh, P. S. D. (2010), 'The third phase of Singapore's multiculturalism', in Tan Tarn How (ed.), *Singapore Perspectives 2010: Home.Heart.Horizon*, Singapore: Institute of Policy Studies and World Scientific.

Göle, N. (2002), 'Islam in public: New visibilities and new imaginaries', *Public Culture*, 14(1): 173–90.

Graham, S. and Weiner, B. (1996), 'Theories and principles of motivation', *Handbook of Educational Psychology*, 4: 63–84.

Gray, M. (2008), 'Explaining conspiracy theories in modern Arab Middle Eastern political discourse: Some problems and limitations of the literature', *Critique: Critical Middle Eastern Studies*, 17(2): 155–74.

Habermas, J. (1989), *The New Conservatism*, Cambridge, MA: Polity Press.

Hafez, M. M. (2003), *Why Muslims Rebel*, Boulder, CO: Lynne Rienner.

Hall, M. and Jackson, P. T., eds (2007), *Civilizational Identity: The Production and Reproduction of 'civilizations' in International Relations*, London: Macmillan.

Halliday, M. (1996), *Islam and the Myth of Confrontation: Religion and Politics in the Middle East*, New York: St Martin's Press.

Hampsher-Monk, I., Tilmans, K. and van Vree, F. eds (1998), *History of Concepts: Comparative Perspectives*, Amsterdam: Amsterdam University Press.

Haritaworn, J., Tauqir, T. and Erdem, E. (2008), 'Gay imperialism: Gender and sexuality discourse in the war on terror', in A. Kuntsman and M. Esperanza (eds), *Out of Place. Interrogating Silences in Queerness/Raciality*, 71–95, New York: Raw Nerve Books.

Harré, R. (1986), *The Social Construction of Emotions*, Oxford: Oxford University Press.

Haslam, N. (2006), 'Dehumanization: An integrative review', *Personality and Social Psychology Review*, 10(3): 252–64.

Hassan, R. (2008), *Inside Muslim Minds*, Melbourne: Melbourne University Press.

Hauser, M. D. (2006), *Moral Minds: How Nature Designed our Universal Sense of Right and Wrong*, New York: Ecco.

Heelas, P. (2007), 'Emotional talk across cultures', in H. Wulff (ed.), *The Emotions: A Cultural Reader*, 31–6, Oxford: Berg.

Hefner, R. W. (2000), *Civil Islam: Muslims and democratization in Indonesia*, Princeton, NJ: Princeton University Press.

Hekma, G. (2002), 'Imams and homosexuality: A post-gay debate in the Netherlands', *Sexualities*, 5(2): 237–48.

Hetherington, M. and Suhay, E. (2011), 'Authoritarianism, threat, and Americans'usupport for the war on terror', *American Journal of Political Science*, 55(3): 546–60.

Higgins, E. T. (1989), 'Self-discrepancy theory: What patterns of self-beliefs cause people to suffer?' *Advances in Experimental Social Psychology*, 22: 93–136.

Hindelang, M. J., Hirschi, T. and Weis, J. G. (1981), *Measuring Delinquency*, Beverly Hills, CA: Sage Publications.

Hirschkind, C. (2006), *The Ethical Soundscape: Cassette Sermons and Islamic Counterpublics*, Columbia: Columbia University Press.

Hodges, A. and Nilep, C., eds (2007), *Discourse, War and Terrorism*, Amsterdam: John Benjamins Publishing.

Hoeveler, D. (2006), 'The Female Captivity Narrative: Blood, Water, and Orientalism', in D. L. Hoeveler and J. Cass (eds), *Interrogating Orientalism: Contextual Approaches and Pedagogical Practices*, 46–71, Columbus: Ohio State University Press.

Hofstadter, R. (1965), 'The paranoid style in American politics', in R. Hofstadter (ed.), *The Paranoid Style in American Politics and Other Essays*, 3–40, Cambridge, MA: Harvard University Press.

Holloway, D. (2008), *9/11 and the War on Terror*, Edinburgh: Edinburgh University Press.

Huntington S. (1993), 'The clash of civilizations?', *Foreign Affairs*, 72 (3): 22–8.

Huntington, S. (1996), *The Clash of Civilizations and the Remaking of World Order*, New York: Simon & Schuster.

Hurrell, A. (2005), 'Pax Americana or the empire of insecurity?', *International Relations of The Asia Pacific*, 5(2): 153–76.

Ibn Khaldūn, A. (1986), *The Muqaddimah: An Introduction to History*, trans. from Arabic by: Franz Rosenthal, London: Routledge & Kegan Paul.

Ibn Manzur, Abu al-Faraj (1968), *Lisan al-Arab*, Beirut: Dar Sadir.

Inglehart, R. and Norris, P. (2003), 'The true clash of civilizations', *Foreign Policy*, 135: 62–70.

Ismail, B. (2010), 'Ban the burqa? France votes yes', *Middle East Quarterly*, 17(4): 47–55.

Izard, C. (1977), *Human Emotions*, New York: Plenum Press.

Izustsu, T. (1966), *Ethico-religious Concepts in the Quran*, Montreal: Mcgill University Press.

Jahoda, G. (1999), 'Images of savages: Ancient roots of modern prej- udice in western culture', London: Routledge & Kegan Paul.

Jang, S. J. and Johnson, B. R. (2003), 'Strain, negative emotions, and deviant coping among African Americans: A test of general strain theory', *Journal of Quantitative Criminology*, 19: 79–105.

Jikeli, G. and Allouche-Benayoun, J., eds (2013), 'Perceptions of the holocaust in Europe and Muslim communities', in *Sources, Comparisons and Educational Challenges*, vol. 5, Dordrecht, Heidelberg, New York, London: Springer.

Jivraj, S. and de Jong, A. (2011), 'The dutch homo-emancipation policy and its silencing effects on queer Muslims', *Feminist Legal Studies*, 19(2): 143–58.

Johnson, R. (1979), *Juvenile Delinquency and its Origin*, Cambridge: Cambridge University Press.

Kahf, M. (1999), 'Western representations of the Muslim woman: From termagant to odalisque', Austin, TX: University of Texas Press.

Kam, C. D. and Kinder, D. R. (2007), 'Terror and ethnocentrism: Foundations of American support for the war on terrorism', *Journal of Politics*, 69(2): 320–38.

Katz, R. and Kern, M. (2006), Online news story, http://www.washingtonpost. com/wp-dyn/content/article/2006/03/25/AR2006032500020.html.

Keeley, B. L. (1999), 'Of conspiracy theories', *Journal of Philosophy*, 96(3): 109–26.

Kelman, H. C. (1976), 'Violence without restraint: Reflections on the dehumanization of victims and victimizers', in G. M. Kren and L. H. Rappoport (eds), *Varieties of Psychohistory*, 282–314, New York: Springer.

Kepel, G. (2004), *The War for Muslim Minds: Islam and the West*, Cambridge, MA: Harvard University Press.

Khan, M. M. (2001), 'The political philosophy of Islamic resurgence', *Cultural Dynamics*, 13(2): 211–29.

Kofta, M. and Sedek, G. (2005), 'Conspiracy stereotypes of Jews during systemic transformation in Poland', *International Journal of Sociology*, 35: 40–64.

Koselleck, R. (1985), 'Begriffgeschichte and social history', in R. Koselleck (ed.), *Futures Past: On the Semantics of Historical Time*, 73–91, Cambridge, MA: MIT Press.

Kringelbach, M. L. (2004), 'Emotions', in R. L. Gregory (ed.), *The Oxford Companion to the Mind*, 287–90, Oxford: Oxford University Press.

Krohn, M. D., Akers, R. L., Radosevich, M. J. and Lanza KAduce, L. O. N. N. (1980), 'Social status and deviance', *Criminology*, 18(3): 303–18.

Kumar, D. (2010), 'Framing Islam: The resurgence of orientalism during the Bush II era', *Journal of Communication Inquiry*, 34(3): 254–77.

Kumar, D. (2012), *Islamophobia: And the Politics of Empire*, Chicago: Haymarket Books.

Kundnani, A. (2012), 'Multiculturalism and its discontents: Left, Right and liberal', *European Journal of Cultural Studies*, 15(2): 155–66.

Kuo, C. C. (2013), 'The failure of multiculturalism: A challenge for the European Union', *Tamkang Journal of International Affairs*, 16(3): 55–74.

Kupchan, C. A. (2002), *The End of the American Era*, New York: Knopf.

Kuper, A. (1999), *Culture: The Anthropologists' Account*, Cambridge, MA: Harvard University Press.

LaFree, G. and Dugan, L. (2004), 'How does studying terrorism compare to studying crime?', *Sociology of Crime, Law and Deviance*, 5: 53–74.

LaFree, G. and Morris, N. A. (2012), 'Does legitimacy matter? Attitudes toward anti-American violence in Egypt, Morocco, and Indonesia', *Crime & Delinquency*, 58(5): 689–719.

Laqueur, T. (1990), *Making Sex: Body and Gender from the Greeks to Freud*, Cambridge, MA: Harvard University Press.

Lazar, A. and Lazar, M. (2004), 'The discourse of the new world order: "Out-casting" the double face of threat', *Discourse & Society*, 15(2–3): 223–42.

Lecker, M. (2004), *The 'Constitution of Medina': Muhammad's First Legal Document*, Princeton, NJ: Darwin Press.

Leiken, R. S. (2005), 'Europe's angry Muslims', *Foreign Affairs*, 3: 120–35.

Lewis, B. (1990), 'The roots of Muslim rage', *The Atlantic Monthly*, 266(3): 47–60.

Lewis, B. (2003), *The Crisis of Islam: Holy War and Unholy Terror*, New York: Modern Library.

Lewis, P. (2007), *Young, British and Muslim*, London: Continuum International Publishing Group.

Leyens, J. Ph., Rodriguez, A. P., Rodriguez, R. T., Gaunt, R., Paladino, P. M., Vaes, J., et al. (2001), 'Psychological essentialism and the attribution of uniquely human emotions to ingroups and out- groups', *European Journal of Social Psychology*, 31: 395–411.

Leyens, J. Ph., Cortes, B. P., Demoulin, S., Dovidio, J. F., Fiske, S. T., Gaunt, R., et al. (2003), 'Emotional prejudice, essentialism, and nationalism', *European Journal of Social Psychology*, 33: 704–17.

Lindekilde, L., Mouritsen, P. and Zapata-Barrero, R. (2009), 'The Muhammad cartoons controversy in comparative perspective', *Ethnicities*, 9(3): 291–313.

Link, B. G. and Phelan, J. C. (2013), 'Labeling and stigma', in Carol S. Aneshensel, Jo C. Phelan and Alex Bierman (eds), *Handbook of the Sociology of Mental Health*, 525–41, Dordrecht, The Netherlands: Springer.

Lupton, D. (1998), *The Emotional Self: A Sociocultural Explanation*, Oxford: Oxford University Press.

Lutz, C. (2007), 'Emotion, thought and estrangement: Emotion as a cultural category', in H. Wulff (ed.), *The Emotions: A Cultural Reader*, 19–29, Oxford: Berg.

Lyon, M. (1998), 'The limitations of cultural constructionism in the study of emotions', in G. Bendelow and S. J. Williams (eds), *Emotions in Social Life*, 39–60, London: Routledge.

Maddox, G. (2003), 'The "Crusade" against evil: Bush's fundamentalism', *Australian Journal of Politics and History*, 49(3): 398–411.

Mahmood, S. (2006), 'Secularism, hermeneutics, and empire: The politics of Islamic reformation', *Public Culture*, 18(2): 323.

Mahmood, S. (2011), *Politics of Piety: The Islamic Revival and the Feminist Subject*, Princeton: Princeton University Press.

Ma'oz, M., ed. (2012), *Muslim Attitudes to Jews and Israel: The Ambivalences of Rejection, Antagonism, Tolerance and Cooperation*, London: Sussex Academic Press.

Malik, M. (2009), 'Anti-Muslim prejudice in the West, past and present: An introduction', *Patterns of Prejudice*, 43(3–4): 207–12.

Malik, M., ed. (2010), *Anti-Muslim Prejudice: Past and Present*, London: Routledge.

Mamdani, M. (2004), *Good Muslim, Bad Muslim*, New York: Pantheon Books.

Mansour, A. A. (1982), *Hudud Crimes. Islamic Criminal Justice System*, 196–201, New York: Oceana

Marcus, E. (2002), *Making Gay History: The Half-century Fight for Lesbian and Gay Equal Rights*, 10, New York, NY: Perennial.

Marks, S. R. (1974), 'Durkheim's theory of anomie', *American Journal of Sociology*, 80(2): 329–69.

Marranci, G. (2004), 'Multiculturalism, Islam and the clash of civilisations theory: Rethinking Islamophobia', *Culture and Religion*, 5(1): 105–17.

Marranci, G. (2006), *Jihad Beyond Islam*, London: Berg.

Marranci. G. (2007), 'From the Ethos of justice to the ideology of justice: Understanding radical views of Scottish Muslims', in T. Abbas (ed.), *Islamic Political Radicalism: A European Perspective*, 131–44, Edinburgh: Edinburgh University Press.

Marranci, G. (2008), 'British Muslims and the British State', in B. Turner (ed.), *Religious Diversity and Civil Society: A Comparative Analysis*, 123–41, Oxford: Bardwell Press.

Marranci, G. (2009), *Faith, Ideology and Fear: Muslim Identities within and Beyond Prisons*, London and New York: Continuum Books.

Marranci, G. (2011), 'Integration, minorities and the rhetoric of civilization: The case of British Pakistani Muslims in the UK and Malay Muslims in Singapore', *Ethnic and Racial Studies*, 34(5): 814–32.

Mazerolle, P. and Piquero, A. (1997), 'Violent responses to strain: An examination of conditioning influences', *Violence and Victims*, 12: 323–43.

Mazerolle, P. and Maahs, J. (2000), 'General strain and delinquency: An alternative examination of conditioning influences', *Justice Quarterly*, 17: 753–78.

Mazlish, B. (2004), *Civilization and its Contents*, Stanford, CA: Stanford University Press.

McCauley, C. and Stellar, J. (2010), 'US Muslims after 9/11: Poll trends 2001-2007', *Perspectives on Terrorism*, 3(3): 35–46.

McCrisken, T. (2011), 'Ten years on: Obama's war on terrorism in rhetoric and practice', *International Affairs*, 87(4): 781–801.

Mcdonald, M. (2005), 'Be alarmed? Australia's anti-terrorism kit and the politics of security', *Global Change, Peace & Security*, 17(2): 171–89.

Meade, R. C. (1990), *Red Brigades: The Story of Italian Terrorism*, Basingstoke: Macmillan.

Mepschen, P., Duyvendak, J. W. and Tonkens, E. H. (2010), 'Sexual politics, orientalism and multicultural citizenship in the Netherlands', *Sociology*, 44(5): 962–79.

Merolla, J. and Zechmeister, E. (2009), *Democracy at Risk: How Terrorist Threats Affect the Public*, Chicago: University of Chicago Press.

Merton, R. K. (1938), 'Social structure and anomie', *American Sociological Review*, 3(5): 672–82.

Merton, R. K., ed. (1968), *Social Theory and Social Structure*, Glencoe, IL: Simon and Schuster.

Merton, R. K. (1995), 'Opportunity structure: The emergence, diffusion and differentiation of a sociological concept, 1930s–1950s', in F. Adler and W. S. Laufer (eds), *Advances in Criminological Theory, vol. 10, The Legacy of Anomie Theory*, 3–78, New Brunswick, NJ: Transaction Publishers.

Merton, R. K. (1997a), 'On the evolving synthesis of differential association and anomie theory: A perspective from the sociology of science', *Criminology*, 35(3): 517–25.

Merton, R. K. (1997b), 'Foreword', in N. Passas and R. Agnew (eds), *The Future of Anomie Theory*, ix–xii, Boston: Northeastern University Press.

Mill, J. and Thomas, W. (1975), *The History of British India, Classics of British Historical Literature*, Chicago: University of Chicago Press.

Milton, K. (2002), *Loving Nature*, London: Routledge.

Milton, K. (2007), 'Emotion (or, life, the Universe, everything)', in H. Wulff (ed.), *The Emotions: A Cultural Reader*, 198–211, Oxford: Berg.

Milton, K. and Svasek, M. (2005), *Mixed Emotions: Anthropological Studies of Feeling*, Oxford: Berg.

Mirza, H. S. (2013a), 'Embodying the veil: Muslim women and gendered Islamophobia in "New Times"', in Zehavit Gross, Lynn Davies and Al-Khansaa Diab (eds), *Gender, Religion and Education in a Chaotic Postmodern World*, 303–16, Dordrecht, The Netherlands: Springer.

Mirza, H. S. (2013b), 'Muslim women and gender stereotypes in "New Times": From multiculturalism to Islamophobia', in Nisha Kapoor, Virinder S. Kalra and James Rhodes (eds), *The State of Race,* 96–120, Hampshire: Palgrave Macmillan.

Modood, T. (2013), *Multiculturalism*, Hoboken: John Wiley & Sons.

Moon, B. and Morash, M. (2004), 'Adaptation of theory for alternative cultural contexts: Agnew's general strain theory in South Korea', *Journal of International and Comparative Criminal Justice*, 28: 77–104.

Mosquera, P. M. R. (2013), 'In the name of honor: On virtue, reputation and violence', *Group Processes & Intergroup Relations*, 16(3): 271–8.

Musallam, A. (2005), *From Secularism to Jihad: Sayyid Qutb and the Foundations of Radical Islamism*, Westport, CT: Praeger.

Nagra, B. and Peng, I. (2013), 'Has multiculturalism really failed? A Canadian Muslim perspective', *Religions*, 4(4): 603–20.

Navarro, L. (2010), Islamophobia and sexism: Muslim women in the western mass media', *Human Architecture: Journal of the Sociology of Self-Knowledge*, 8(2): 10.

Netton, R. I (1992), *Popular Dictionary of Islam*, London: Curzon Press.

Newheiser, A., Farias, M. and Tausch, N. (2011), 'The functional nature of conspiracy beliefs: Exam- ining the underpinnings of belief in the Da Vinci code conspiracy', *Personality and Individual Differences*, 51: 1007–11.

Noorani, A. G. (2002), *Islam and Jihad: Prejudice Versus Reality*, London: Zed Book.

O'Tuathail, G. (1996), *Critical Geopolitics: The Politics of Writing Global Space*, 247, Minneapolis, MN: University of Minnesota Press.

Office of Mrs Bush (2001), 'Radio Address by Mrs Bush', 17 November, http://www.whitehouse.gov/news/releases/2001/11/20011117.html (accessed 12 February 2012).

Oliver, K. (2013), *Women as Weapons of War: Iraq, Sex, and the Media*, New York: Columbia University Press.

Orrù, M. (1987), *Anomie: History and Meanings*, Boston: Allen & Unwin.

Ozyurt, S. (2013), 'Negotiating multiple identities, constructing Western–Muslim selves in the Netherlands and the United States', *Political Psychology*, 34(2): 239–63.

Panagopoulos, C. (2006), 'The polls-trends Arab and Muslim Americans and Islam in the aftermath of 9/11', *Public Opinion Quarterly*, 70(4): 608–24.

Pangle, T. L. (2006), *Leo Strauss: An Introduction to his Thought and Intellectual Legacy*, Baltimore: Johns Hopkins University Press.

Parish, J. and Parker, M. (2001), *The Age of Anxiety: Conspiracy Theory and the Human Sciences*, Oxford: Blackwell.

Parkinson, B. (1995), *Ideas and Realities of Emotion*, International Library of Psychology, London: Routledge.

Parpart, J. L. (1988), 'Women and the State in Africa', in Donald Rothchild and Naomi Chazan (eds), *The Precarious Balance: State and Society in Africa*, 208–30, Boulder, CO and London: Westview Press.

Passas, N. and Agnew, R., ed. (1997), *The Future of Anomie Theory*, Boston: Northeastern University Press.

Pauly, Jr, R. J. (2013), *Islam in Europe: Integration or Marginalization?*, Aldershot: Ashgate Publishing, Ltd.

Pew Research Centre Global Attitude Project 'Muslim-Western Tension Persists', 21 July 2011, http://www.pewglobal.org/files/2011/07/Pew-Global-Attitudes-Muslim-Western-Relations-FINAL-FOR-PRINT-July-21-2011.pdf.

Pious, R. M. (2011), 'Prerogative power in the Obama administration: Continuity and change in the war on terrorism', *Presidential Studies Quarterly*, 41(2): 263–90.

Pipes, D. (1996), *The Hidden Hand: Middle East Fears of Conspiracy*, London: Macmillan Press.

Pipes, D. (1997), *Conspiracy: How the Paranoid Style Flourishes and Where It Comes From*, New York: Free Press.

Pipes, D. (2002), *Militant Islam reaches America*, New York: W.W. Norton.

Pippidi, M. and Mindreuta, D. (2002), 'Was Huntington right? Testing cultural legacies and the civilization border', *International Politics*, 39(2): 193–213.

Piquero, N. L. and Sealock, M. D. (2000), 'Generalizing general strain theory: An examination of an offending population', *Justice Quarterly*, 17: 449–84.

Poynting, S. (2006), 'What caused the Cronulla riot', *Race & Class*, 48(1): 85–92.

Poynting, S. (2013), 'The crises of multiculturalism: Racism in a neoliberal age', *Journal of Multilingual and Multicultural Development*, 34(3): 299–301.

Poynting, S., Noble, G., Tabar, P. and Collins, J. (2004), *Bin Laden in the Suburbs: Criminalising the Arab other*, Sydney: Sydney Institute of Criminology.

Puar, J. (2007), *Terrorist Assemblages. Homonationalism in Queer Times*, Durham, NC: Duke University Press.

Rabinow, P. (1997), *Reflections on Filedwork in Morocco*, Berkeley: University of California Press.

Rajan, R. S. (2004), *Real and Imagined Women: Gender, Culture and Postcolonialism*, Chicago: Routledge.

Ramusack, B. (1990), 'Cultural missionaries, maternal imperialists, feminist allies: British women activists in India, 1865–1945', *Women's Studies International Forum*, 13(4): 302–21.

Randall, M. (2011), *9/11 and the Literature of Terror*, Chicago: Edinburgh University Press.

Rashid, N. (2013), 'Giving the silent majority a stronger voice? Initiatives to empower Muslim women as part of the UK's "War on Terror"', *Ethnic and Racial Studies*, (ahead-of-print), 1–16.

Rausch, S. and LaFree, G. (2007), 'The growing importance of criminology in the study of terrorism', *The Criminologist*, 32(6): 1, 3–5.

Reynolds, N. (1993), 'Ethos as location: New sites for understanding discursive authority', *Rhetoric Review*, 11(2): 325–38.

Riley, D. (1988), *'Am I That Name?' Feminism and the Category of 'Women' in History*, Basingstoke: Macmillan.

Riley, R. L., Mohanty, C. T. and Pratt, M. B. (2008), *Feminism and War: Confronting US Imperialism*, London: Zed.

Rina, D. (1996), 'The Abbasid construction of the jahiliyya: Cultural authority in the making', *Studia Islamica*, 83: 38–49.

Roberts, J. M. (1972), *The Mythology of the Secret Society*, New York: Scribner.

Roose, J. M. (2013), 'Contesting Islam through the 2012 Sydney protests: An analysis of post-protest political discourse amongst Australian Muslims', *Islam and Christian–Muslim Relations*, (ahead-of-print), 1–21.

Rosaldo, M. Z. (1984), 'Toward an anthropology of self and feeling', in R. A. Shweder and R. A. LeVine (eds), *Culture Theory: Essays on Mind, Self, and Emotion*, 137–57, Cambridge: Cambridge University Press.

Rosenfeld, R. (2002), 'Why criminologists should study terrorism', *The Criminologist*, 27(6): 1, 3–4.

Rosenfeld, R. (2004), 'Terrorism and criminology', *Sociology of Crime, Law and Deviance*, 5: 19–32.

Roy, O. (2006), *Globalized Islam: The Search for a New ummah*, New York: Columbia University Press.

Roy, O. (2013), 'Secularism and Islam: The theological predicament', *The International Spectator*, 48(1): 5–19.

Rushdie, S. (1998), *The Satanic Verses*, London: Vintage.

Sacks, K. (1982), 'An overview of women and power in Africa', in Jean O'Barr (ed.), *Perspectives on Power: Women in Africa, Asia and Latin America*, 1–120, Durham, NC: Duke University, Center for International Studies.

Sandberg, S. (2013), 'Are self-narratives strategic or determined, unified or fragmented? Reading Breivik's Manifesto in light of narrative criminology', *Acta Sociologica*, 56(1): 69–83.

Sanjakdar, F. (2013), 'Educating for sexual difference? Muslim teachers' conversations about homosexuality', *Sex Education*, 13(1): 16–29.

Sankar, L. V. (2013), 'Malaysian editorials on the Allah issue: A critical discourse study', *Critical Inquiry in Language Studies*, 10(1): 31–61.

Scott, J. W. (2005), 'Symptomatic politics the banning of Islamic head scarves in French public schools', *French Politics, Culture & Society*, 23(3): 106–27.

Seddon, M. S. (2001), 'Locating the perpetuation of "otherness": Negating British Islam', *Encounters*, 8(2): 139–61.

Seib, P. (2004), 'The news media and the "Clash of civilizations"', *Journal of the US Army War College*, 34(4): 71–85.

Shafir, G., Meade, E. and Aceves, W. J., eds (2012), *Lessons and Legacies of the War on Terror: From Moral Panic to Permanent War*, London: Routledge.

Shaheen, J. G. (2000), 'Hollywood's Muslim Arabs', *The Muslim World*, 90(1–2): 22–42.

Shepard, W. (2001), 'The age of ignorance', in J. D. McAuliffe (ed.), *Encyclopaedia of the Qur'an*, Leiden: Brill.

Shepard, W. (2003), 'Sayyid Qutb's doctrine of jahiliyya', *International Journal of Middle East Studies*, 35(4): 521–45.

Shryock, A., ed. (2010), *Islamophobia/Islamophilia: Beyond the Politics of Enemy and Friend*, Chicago: Indiana University Press.

Silverstein, B. (2003), 'Islam and modernity in Turkey: Power, tradition and historicity in the European provinces of the Muslim world', *Anthropological Quarterly*, 76(3): 497–517.

Simpson, J. A. and Weiner, E. S. C. (1989), *The Oxford English Dictionary*, Oxford: Clarendon Press.

Soares, B. F. and Otayek, R. (2007), *Islam and Muslim Politics in Africa*, London: Palgrave Macmillan.

Soares, B. and Osella, F. (2009), 'Islam, politics, anthropology', *Journal of the Royal Anthropological Institute*, 15(1): 1–23.

Solomon, R. C. (1989), 'The emotions of justice', *Social Justice Research*, 3(4): 345–74.

Solomon, R. C. (1990), *A Passion for Justice: Emotions and the Origins of the Social Contract*, Reading, MA: Addison-Wesley Pub. Co.

Spencer, R. (2005), *The Myth of Islamic Tolerance: How Islamic Law Treats Non-Muslims*, Amherst, NY: Prometheus Books.

Spencer, R. (2007), *Religion of Peace?: Why Christianity Is and Islam Isn't*, Washington, DC: Regnery Pub.

Spencer, R. (2008), *Stealth Jihad*, Chicago: Regnery Publishing.

Sprinzak, E. (1995), 'Right wing terrorism in a comparative perspective: The case of split delegitimization', *Terrorism and Political Violence*, 7(1): 17–43.

Spruyt, B. J. (2007), '"Can't we discuss this?" Liberalism and the challenge of Islam in the Netherlands', *Orbis*, 51(2): 313–29.

Starobinski, J. (1993), *Blessings in Disguise*, Cambridge, MA: Harvard University Press.

Stempel, C., Hargrove, T. and Stempel, G. H. (2007), 'Media use, social structure, and belief in 9/11 conspiracy theories', *Journalism & Mass Communication Quarterly*, 84(2): 353–72.

Stone, J. and Cooper, J. (2001), 'A self-standards model of cognitive dissonance', *Journal of Experimental Social Psychology*, 37: 228–43.

Strobel, M. (1991), *European Women and the Second British Empire*, Bloomington, IN: Indiana University Press.

Struch, N. and Schwartz, S. H. (1989), 'Intergroup aggression: Its pre- dictors and distinctness from in-group bias', *Journal of Person- ality and Social Psychology*, 56: 364–73.

Swami, V., Chamorro-Premuzic, T. and Furnham, A. (2010), Unanswered questions: A preliminary investigation of personality and individual differ- ence predictors of 9/11 conspiracist beliefs', *Applied Cognitive Psychology*, 24: 749–61.

Swami, V., Coles, R., Stieger, S., Pietschnig, J., Furnham, A., Rehim, S., et al. (2011), 'Conspiracist ideation in Britain and Austria: evidence of a monological belief system and associations between individual psychological differences and real- world and fictitious conspiracy theories', *British Journal of Psychology*, 102: 443–63.

Sweeten, G., Piquero, A. R. and Steinberg, L. (2013), 'Age and the explanation of crime, revisited', *Journal of Youth and Adolescence*, 42(6): 921–38.

Tessler, M. (2003), 'Arab and Muslim political attitudes: Stereotypes and evidence from survey research', *International Studies Perspectives*, 4(2): 175–81.

Tessler, M. and Robbins, M. D. (2007), 'What leads some ordinary Arab men and women to approve of terrorist acts against the United States?', *Journal of Conflict Resolution*, 51(2): 305–28.

Thexton, M. (2006), *What Happened to the Hippy man?: Hijack Hostage Survivor*, London: Lanista Partners.

Thornberry, T. P. and Farnworth, M. (1982), 'Social correlates of criminal involvement: Further evidence on the relationship between social status and criminal behavior', *American Sociological Review*, 47: 505–18.

Timmerman, G. (2013), 'Femen: Une nouvelle forme de militantisme? À quel prix et avec quelle efficacité?', *Analyses & Étudesn Société*, 7: 1–14.

Todorov, T. (2010), *The Fear of Barbarians: Beyond the Clash of Civilizations*, Chicago: University of Chicago Press.

Tomaka, J. and Blascovich, J. (1994), 'Effects of justice beliefs on cognitive appraisal of and subjective physiological, and behavioral responses to potential stress', *Journal of Personality and Social Psychology*, 67(4): 732–40.

Towns. A. (2007), 'The status of women and the ordering of human societies along the stages of civilization', in M. Hall and P. T. Jackson (eds), *Civilizational Identity: The Production and Reproduction of "Civilizations" in International Relations*, 167–80, New York: Palgrave MacMillan.

Towns, A. (2009), 'The status of women as a standard of "Civilization"', *European Journal of International Relations*, 15(4): 681–706.

Tufail, W. and Poynting, S. (2013), 'A common "outlawness": Criminalisation of Muslim minorities in the UK and Australia', *International Journal for Crime, Justice and Social Democracy*, 2(3): 43–54.

Turner, B. S. (2002), 'Sovereignty and emergency political theology, Islam and American conservatism', *Theory, Culture & Society*, 19(4): 103–19.

Umpleby, S. A. (1997), 'Cybernetics of conceptual systems', *Cybernetics & Systems*, 28(8): 635–51.

Van der Veer, P. (2006), 'Pim Fortuyn, Theo van Gogh, and the politics of tolerance in the Netherlands', *Public Culture*, 18(1): 111–24.

Van Veen, V., Krug, M. K., Schooler, J. W. and Carter, C. S. (2009), 'Neural activity predicts attitude change in cognitive dissonance', *Nature Neuroscience*, 12(11): 1469–74.

Varisco, D. M. (2005), *Islam Obscured: The Rhetoric of Anthropological Representation*, New York: Palgrave Macmillan.

Von Knop, K. (2007), 'The female Jihad: Al Qaeda's women', *Studies in Conflict & Terrorism*, 30(5): 397–414.

Von Sommer, A. and Zwemmer, S. (1907), *Our Muslims Sisters: A cry of Need From Lands of Darkness*, New York: Fleming H Revell Company.

Weber, M. (1978), *Economy and Society*, 2 vols, Berkeley: University of California Press.

Weber, M., Baehr, P. R. and Wells, G. C., eds (2002), *The Protestant Ethic and the "spirit" of Capitalism and other Writings*, London: Penguin.

Wege, C. A. (1991), 'The Abu Nidal organization', *Studies in Conflict & Terrorism*, 14(1): 59–66.

Weinberg, L. and Eubank, W. L. (1988), 'Neo-fascist and far left terrorists in Italy: Some biographical observations', *British Journal of Political Science*, 18(04): 531–49.

Weinner, P. P. (1973), *Dictionary of the History of Ideas*, New York: Charles.

Weiss, H. M., Suckow, K. and Cropanzano, R. (1999), 'Effects of justice conditions on discrete emotions', *Journal of Applied Psychology*, 84(5): 786.

Wekker, G. (2009), *Van homo nostalgie en betere tijden: Multiculturaliteit en postkolonialiteit*, Amsterdam: Stichting George Mosse.

Wentworth, W. M. and Yardley, D. (1994), 'Deep sociality: A bioevolutionary perspective on the sociology of human emotions', in D. Franks, W. M. Wentworth and J. Ryan (eds), *Social Perspectives on Emotions*, vol. 2, 21–55, Greenwich, CT: JAI Press.

West, H. G. and Sanders, T., eds (2003), *Transparency and Conspiracy: Ethnographies of Suspicion in the New World Order*, Durham, NC: Duke University Press.

White, J. B. (2011), *Islamist Mobilization in Turkey: A Study in Vernacular Politics*, Washington, DC: University of Washington Press.

Williamson, M. and Khiabany, G. (2010), 'UK: The veil and the politics of racism', *Race & Class*, 52(2): 85–96.

Wood, N. (1991), *Cicero's Social and Political Thought*, Berkeley, CA: University of California.

Ye'or, B. (2002), *Islam and Dhimmitude: Where Civilizations Collide*, Madison, NJ: Fairleigh Dickinson University Press.

Ye'or, B. (2004), *Eurabia: The Euro-Arab Axis*, Rutherford, NJ: Fairleigh Dickinson University Press.

Yip, A. K. T. (2004), 'Negotiating space with family and kin in identity construction: The Narratives of British non-heterosexual Muslims', *Sociological Review*, 52(3): 336–49.

Yonah, A. and Pluchinsky, A. D. eds (1992), *Europe's Red Terrorists: The Fighting Communist Organizations*, Washington, DC: Frank Cass Publishers.

Yousafzai, M. and Lamb, C. (2013), *I am Malala: The Story of the Girl Who Stood Up for Education and was Shot by the Taliban*, London: Hachette.

Zonis, M. and Joseph, C. M. (1994), 'Conspiracy thinking in the middle east', *Political Psychology*, 15: 443–59.

Index